HELLO, FROM THE OTHER SIDE

BY

INTERNATIONAL MEDIUM

VAL WILLIAMS

MINISTER OF THE SNU, TUTOR AT THE ARTHUR FINDLAY
COLLEGE,

SNU HEALER, HYPNOTHERAPIST CM.HSP. LSSNU.

FOUNDER OF VAL WILLIAMS ACADEMY FOR MEDIUMSHIP

CONTENTS

SOMEONE DOES CARE. LOCKDOWN 2020-Val Williams 31st March.

What do I miss, what do I need?

Connecting with people, no matter their creed,

People are hurting, some more than others,

Some are missing fathers and some their mothers.

Isolation is easy when you have no pain

For stress and exhaustion it offers a gain,

But for those who are lonely and have no-one to care

They need to remember that God hears their prayer

.....

So when you are busy or just carrying on,

Remember the people who are living on their own

Their contact with people is vital you see

So they aren't forgotten or think they will be,

A phone call, a letter, a little hello

Will brighten the soul of one who's alone

So come on you people who have love in your life

Remind the widower he still has a wife.

.....

Remind the widow she is not alone

Her husband still loves her, though he cannot be shown.

THANKS

My grateful thanks to everyone who helped this book to become a reality. I had started to write it over 10 years ago and had abandoned it. Due to many complications in the writing and re-writing of this version there are times when other people's way of writing overlaps mine. I am truly grateful to everyone for their input, encouragement and love.

My special thanks to:

Pete Finlay for the beautiful cover.

...

Penny, for being inspired by Spirit to give me the title.

...

Sheelagh and Martin for recording some of my stories.

...

Trish, Andrea, Margaret, Maddie and Shaun for proofreading and formatting.

...

I will always be grateful to a stranger, who approached me in Portsmouth Temple, because she motivated me to get back to writing the book and finishing it.

...

To all the people who allowed me to tell their stories, many names have been changed to preserve privacy but every story is true.

...

Most of all, to the Spirit people who trusted me with their messages of evidence, which brought hope for the future, peace to the trouble souls of their loved ones, emotional closure where necessary, all this leaving us in no doubt that we will NEVER be separated from those we have loved they are no further away than a phone call to the other side of life, which we call the Spirit world.

...

Due to the ongoing nature of the interaction with Spirit I already have enough material for a third book, which will also include many teaching aids to help developing mediums.

INTRODUCTION

IT IS NOW 20 YEARS SINCE I WROTE MY FIRST BOOK ABOUT MEDIUMSHIP, THE SPIRIT WORLD, MY CONNECTIONS WITH SPIRIT AND THE WONDROUS WAYS IN WHICH SPIRIT MAKE THEIR CONTACTS, THROUGH MEDIUMSHIP, TO LOVED ONES LEFT BEHIND.

MEDIUMS ARE OFTEN ACCUSED OF PREYING ON VULNERABLE PEOPLE, NOT ALLOWING SPIRIT PEOPLE TO REST AND MANY OTHER SUCH SILLY THINGS. THE TRUTH IS THAT IT IS THE SPIRIT PEOPLE WHO CHOOSE WHEN AND HOW TO BRING THEIR TRUTHS OF LIFE AFTER DEATH TO THEIR LOVED ONES WHO ARE STILL LIVING AND, IN SO MANY CASES, STILL GRIEVING AND UNABLE TO MOVE FORWARD WITH THEIR LIVES IN THIS PHYSICAL WORLD.

GRIEVING NATURALLY TAKES MANY FORMS, MUCH OF IT BEING DEPENDANT ON HOW, WHY AND WHEN A LOVED ONE HAS PASSED. MEDIUMSHIP BY ITS NATURAL CONNECTION BETWEEN THE TWO WORLDS SO OFTEN BRINGS EMOTIONAL CLOSURE AND GREATER UNDERSTANDING TO THOSE "LEFT BEHIND." INDEED MANY LOVED ONES STILL LIVING IN THE PHYSICAL WORLD FEEL IT IS ALMOST IMPOSSIBLE TO MOVE FORWARD UNTIL THEY KNOW THEIR LOVED ONES ARE NOW SAFE, AT PEACE, AND WITH LOVED ONES IN THE SPIRIT WORLD.

I HAVE LOST COUNT OF THE NUMBER OF TIMES SOMEONE HAS COME FOR A PRIVATE READING, THEIR SOLE NEED BEING TO KNOW THAT THEIR LOVED ONE WILL STILL BE WAITING FOR THEM WHEN THEY, TOO, PASS TO SPIRIT. ONCE THEY HAVE RECEIVED THE MESSAGE THAT THE LOVED ONE WILL BE WAITING FOR THEM IT IS OFTEN THE CASE THAT THOSE STILL IN THE PHYSICAL WORLD MAY HAVE NEW RELATIONSHIPS, MAY EVEN MARRY AGAIN, KNOWING THAT TO DO SO WILL NOT CAUSE A SOUL CONNECTION TO THE ONE THEY LOST TO BE SEVERED.

A MEDIUM MUST BE A PERSON OF INTEGRITY,

COMPASSION, EMPATHY AND UNDERSTANDING BECAUSE EVERYONE WHO IS SEEKING EVIDENCE OF LIFE AFTER DEATH HAS THEIR OWN REASON FOR WISHING THE ONGOING CONTACT WITH THOSE THEY LOVED AND THOUGHT THEY HAD LOST.

I ENVY THOSE OF YOU WHO ARE JUST BEGINNING YOUR SEARCH FOR PROOF OF YOUR LOVED ONES CONTINUING PRESENCE BECAUSE THERE IS NOTHING QUITE LIKE THE FIRST CONTACT, WHEN IT IS A GOOD ONE, WHEN IT REASSURES YOU, WHEN YOUR SPIRITUAL AND EMOTIONAL NEEDS ARE SUPPORTED.

ON THE OTHER HAND, THERE ARE THOSE OF YOU WHO HAVE SEARCHED FOR MANY YEARS AND ARE STILL SEARCHING FOR THAT ONE PIECE OF EVIDENCE THAT YOU WILL CONSIDER ABSOLUTE PROOF OF THE REALITY OF LIFE IN THAT OTHER DIMENSION WE CALL THE SPIRIT WORLD.

I AM QUITE SURE THAT NO MATTER YOUR REASON FOR INVESTIGATING, IF YOU KEEP AN OPEN MIND AND HEART BUT APPLY COMMON SENSE TO EVERY COMMUNICATION, YOU WILL BE ABLE TO COMPILE YOUR OWN DOSSIER OF EVIDENCE.

I HOPE THAT SOMETHING YOU WILL READ, IN THIS BOOK, WILL AT LEAST ENCOURAGE YOU TO CARRY ON SEARCHING AND RESEARCHING, FOR TO DO SO IS TO GIVE THE SPIRIT LOVED ONES AN OPEN DOOR, TO ALLOW THEM TO BRING FORWARD THEIR TRUTHS IN THE WAYS THEY CHOOSE.

THERE IS NO DOUBT THAT THERE WILL BE TIMES YOU MAY WISH A PARTICULAR PIECE OF EVIDENCE BUT, REMEMBER THIS, THE SPIRIT WORLD IS AN ENVIRONMENT OF INTELLIGENCE, THE SPIRIT LOVED ONES KNOWING WHAT YOU ACTUALLY NEED.

FOR THOSE NEWLY BEREAVED IT IS IMPORTANT THAT THEY NOT ONLY HAVE EVIDENCE OF THE CONTINUING LIFE OF THEIR OWN LOVED ONE BUT, ALSO, LISTENING TO OTHER

PEOPLE'S MESSAGES CAN OFTEN BRING A LOT OF COMFORT, HEALING AND PEACE.

GOOD MEDIUMS FEEL TRULY HUMBLED WHEN A LOVED ONE FROM SPIRIT ALLOWS THEM TO DELIVER A MESSAGE TO SOMEONE WHO MUST NOW CARRY ON WITHOUT THEM, IN THIS PHYSICAL WORLD.

MY CONCERN, FOR THE FUTURE OF OUR WONDERFUL MEDIUMSHIP, IS THAT THERE ARE NO LONGER SO MANY NATURAL MEDIUMS, AND WHILE WE CAN TRAIN MEDIUMS TO BRING OUT THE BEST OF THEIR MEDIUMSHIP IT IS NOT ENOUGH, AND NEVER HAS BEEN, TO SIMPLY GIVE FACTS AND FIGURES AS EVIDENCE.

I HAVE RECENTLY STARTED A MEDIUMSHIP ACADEMY, WHICH WAS SOMETHING I WAS TOLD TO DO BACK IN THE 1980'S, BY GORDON HIGGINSON AND OTHER MEDIUMS, SOME OF THE BEST OF THEIR DAY. THE WONDERFUL WORKERS FOR THE SPIRIT WORLD TOOK THE TIME TO ENCOURAGE ME AS I TOOK MY VERY FIRST STEPS. ALBERT BEST, A WORLD RENOWNED MEDIUM GAVE ME MY FIRST OPPORTUNITY TO WORK AT WHAT WE THEN CALLED STANSTED HALL. DON GALLOWAY INVITED ME TO WORK FOR HIM, FOR HIS LYNWOOD FELLOWSHIP, AND I NEVER LOOKED BACK.

THE AIM OF THE ACADEMY IS VERY SIMPLE, TO ENCOURAGE TODAY'S MEDIUMS TO KNOW THAT THERE IS A PURE FORM OF SPIRITUAL EVIDENCE. IT IS SO EASY TO ACHIEVE THIS ONCE THE MEDIUM STANDS BACK AND ALLOWS THE SPIRIT COMMUNICATOR TO BRING FORWARD NOT ONLY PIECES OF INFORMATION, BUT THE LOVE, PERSONALITY AND HUMOUR THAT NOT ONLY THE RECIPIENT FEELS BUT, DURING A DEMONSTRATION, OTHER PEOPLE ALSO FEEL.

THAT WAS THE GOOD EVIDENTIAL MEDIUMSHIP I EXPERIENCED WHEN I STARTED ON THIS PATHWAY 40 YEARS AGO, AND I CONSIDER MYSELF LUCKY THAT MY

MEDIUMSHIP HAS PROMOTED THOSE VERY IMPORTANT ASPECTS OF THE SPIRIT PERSONALITY. WHEN YOU HAVE WITNESSED THE TRANSFIGURATION OF QUEENIE NIXON, SEEN THE AMAZING MEDIUMSHIP OF STUART LAWSON, BEEN GIVEN THE NAMES OF ALL YOUR NEIGHBOURS BY ALBERT BEST IT SETS A STANDARD TO WORK TOWARDS.

I HAVE HOPE FOR THE FUTURE OF OUR MEDIUMSHIP AND OUR SPIRITUALISM. I BELIEVE IT IS UP TO THE LONG-STANDING MEDIUMS OF TODAY TO ENCOURAGE, IN EVERY WAY POSSIBLE, NEWLY DEVELOPING MEDIUMS TO WANT TO SIMPLY BE THE BEST INSTRUMENT FOR THE SPIRIT TEACHERS, NOTHING MORE AND NOTHING LESS. TRAINING FOR MEDIUMSHIP IS NOT ABOUT COMPETITION, NOT ABOUT HOW MUCH MONEY CAN BE EARNED FOR DOING IT. THE REWARDS THE SPIRIT WORLD OFFERS TO US CANNOT BE BOUGHT AT ANY PRICE.

SO, I WISH TO SAY TO ALL DEVELOPING MEDIUMS: BE WILLING TO TAKE TIME TO MEDITATE, TO BLEND WITH SPIRIT, TO SIT IN THE POWER, GIVING YOUR SPIRIT TEACHERS TIME TO EVALUATE YOU, THEN THEY WILL KNOW HOW BEST TO HELP YOUR MEDIUMSHIP TO PROGRESS. I HOPE IT IS FOR YOU, AS IT WAS FOR ME, THE MOST EXCITING JOURNEY YOU EVER UNDERTAKE, AND REMEMBER, YOU ARE NEVER ALONE – YOUR SPIRIT TEAM WILL ALWAYS BE WITH YOU. ENJOY THE JOURNEY..................

...

DEDICATION

I am dedicating this book to the friends who have passed over to Spirit during the last 20 years. In particular, I would like to dedicate it to a lady who passed just as she had lived: with absolute dignity and with an enduring love and compassion for the many she put before herself.

Lesley is still missed by everyone who knew her, because she was a breath of fresh air. Kind, funny, generous, she was one of those rare people who was unconditionally loving to those close to her, always willing to help someone in need, and ever-ready to organize a party or spontaneously host an event. Lesley loved to arrange fund-raising events! Even now such events are held, in her memory, to raise money for worthy causes.

I know that the Spirit world is a happier place, because she is there. Despite the fact that Lesley will always be missed, I do hope those she left behind know, as I do, that she would want them to carry on living happy lives, safe in the knowledge that she will always be there for them, now and when they, too, pass to Spirit.

Lesley's illness and death happened very quickly. She had told me that I ought to write a second book and promised to help me edit it. Sadly, her time came before I began to assemble the collection of stories that fill these pages. Still, it gives me some comfort and seems fitting that I started to put pen to paper in the home she loved so much.

I often wonder if she was responsible for sending a young woman to the Portsmouth Temple Spiritualist Church, early in 2019. After the Sunday Service a total stranger approached me and offered to write my second book. I told her that I would have to write my own book and that, in fact, I had started it 10 years previously, but never finished it. The young woman then offered to edit it. When I asked if there was a fee she said "of course not," that she just wanted to help to get it written and published. This is the result and this is why I wondered, initially, if Lesley sent her in my direction, knowing how much my first book "Two Worlds as One" had helped many people.

Lesley loved to entertain and if she wasn't organising a fundraising event, she was hosting a dinner party or tea, entertaining from home. She first invited me to her home many years ago, after I had given her a private reading in the South of England.

When I sat down to continue to write this book, I could feel her presence around me, much like I was preparing for a party. From her home in Spirit, she has undoubtedly kept me on track.

With Lesley in mind, I will share with you a story that she used to enjoy me telling. Lesley always listened to my stories. She had a wonderfully mischievous sense of humour. This particular story always made her smile, no matter how many times she heard it.

...

Whenever I arrived home late in the evening, having travelled back from a service or demonstration, I would call at a local Chinese take-away for my very late dinner. On one occasion, the Chinese lady serving me seemed to want to chat a little more than usual.

Chinese Lady:	You very late tonight
Me:	Yes, I've been working
Chinese Lady:	You work very late. What you do?
Me:	I'm a medium
Chinese lady:	What that mean?
Me:	It means I talk to Spirit
Chinese lady.	Ah, I have other customer who works in brewery
Me:	No, I talk with 'dead people'
Chinese lady:	You want curry sauce?

I can hear Lesley's laughter now, and I can visualise her beautiful smile. I hope you will enjoy these stories of my travels and the people I've met, both those on earth and those in Spirit, as much as she would. If you've suffered as some have, I hope the stories will bring you comfort and assurance that you are not alone. And if you are on a journey, hoping to learn more about the Spirit world I hope some of the examples you will read will show you just how down to earth the journey is and how natural the interaction between the physical world and the Spiritual one.

We are all connected by the simple things in life, like a laugh, a memory, a gift from a loved one, and the love we have shared. I have travelled all over the world, and have felt truly blessed when I have been allowed to share my natural, genuine gift of Mediumship, which has allowed me to meet people from all walks of life.

I come from a hard-working background. I grew up in a small British fishing port, in the North of England. On my mum's side, the family were business people, hoteliers, shop owners, and tailors, etc., from Cornwall. My father was a deep-sea fisherman from a very hard-working family in Fleetwood.

My gifts weren't encouraged as a child. I always felt repressed and was never told that I was good enough, at home or in the grammar school I reluctantly attended. Yet, the Spirit world decided I was good enough to work for them and, in time, proved it to me.
Humility comes from knowing you are good enough to be able to help other people, I believe, and that is what Spirit is able to facilitate. They use physical people like me as their messengers, to re-establish the connection with their loved ones still in this world.

It has been a great honour to work for Spirit, making good friends , many of them becoming as close as family who have become a special part of the tapestry of my life with so many of the threads woven by the Spirit loved ones.

I am eternally grateful to so many who, like Lesley, have taught me that life is to be lived, enjoyed and appreciated.

...

MEETINGS ARRANGED BY SPIRIT
THE THEATRE VISIT

During the past 40 years I have had so many instances of Spirit choosing their medium. There is no such thing as a perfect communication. Mediumship is not an exact science but sometimes it seems as if there is absolutely no doubt that Spirit have organized a meeting between a sitter and a medium.

I was working on one of my regular weeks at the Arthur Findlay College and, for whatever reason, there were very few students on that particular week. I was, therefore, busy for every session, having only 90 minutes off in the whole week.

I was, therefore, not too pleased to be asked to give up my time off because two ladies had telephoned from London asking for readings on that very day. As I was the Course organizer and the only tutor in the building it was necessary for me to do the readings.

Rather begrudgingly I gave up my time out and, with hindsight, I have rarely been as happy as I was to do one of the readings. This was of course, for Lesley to whom this book is dedicated.

My first words to her were "You didn't want to come here today – you have come as an ambassador for someone else" to which she replied "yes" very quietly and definitely not wanting to give anything away. What happened for the next half hour was, to me, a very ordinary sitting but, for her husband when given the details, it was something remarkable.

I remember the Spirit people being his parents, his mother obviously adored Lesley, and the information was very important for a member of the family.

After the reading I did one for Lesley's friend and when I

took her back to the reception area Lesley asked me to speak to her husband on her mobile phone. Oh, I said, is he in London? No, she replied, in Nairobi.

Her husband John asked to speak with me and I chatted with him on the phone. He was very excited about the evidence Lesley had received and spoken to him about, so much so that he invited me to visit them in Nairobi.

I said of course, though I never expected to hear any more from them. I was very surprised to receive, a couple of months later a further invitation and so I arranged to go to Nairobi for ten days only, Lesley making all the travel plans and she very kindly sent me the ticket.

It was the most wonderful ten days, getting to know Lesley and John, being taken to the Masai Mara on Safari, going to Mombasa and being treated like a friend of the family, not there just because I could give Spirit messages. In fact, John insisted I must just enjoy my time there and not do any work, such a treat.

There have been many occasions since that time when I have visited their beautiful home, meeting many of their friends, and always, through ongoing readings for John, getting to know his loved ones more and more.

His mother is a remarkable communicator, not surprising when John told me his mother had, in fact, been a medium herself. She and Lesley, now in Spirit, take it in turns to speak to John, reassuring him they are alright and wishing him to just be happy and always providing new evidence and information.

...

COINCIDENCE OR SPIRIT MANIPULATION?
One of the most remarkable meetings I ever had was with Lesley in London.
I was working at the Arthur Findlay College when the organizer asked who would want to go into London one

evening to see a show, He organized the bus to take everyone and arranged for the tickets to be collected just before the show started.

I said I would give it a miss and so the tickets were ordered and the transport booked. At 2pm on the day of the show one of the students dropped out and so the organizer asked if anyone would want his ticket. For no reason at all I said I would have it. I even surprised myself when the words came out of my mouth, because it had been the last thing on my mind.

We duly boarded the coach, arrived in London and went to the theatre to collect the tickets, over 50 in all. I was asked to look after the tickets for the tutors and translators, then we went for a drink because we were in good time and it would be quite some time before the show was due to start.

Originally the show was to be The Lion King but the organizer changed the show and venue. The one we ultimately saw was a Motown show in a very small theatre. I gave the tickets I had to the translators and mediums, so just had my own when I suddenly needed to go to the bathroom. Looking down the theatre I could see that the row in front of where our seats were was almost empty, so I rushed down, going along the empty row and handed my handbag to the translator sitting in the row behind.

I became aware of the lady who was sitting on my right and felt I should apologise for invading her space. As I looked down she looked up and we were both in shock "Val, what are you doing here?" she asked. "Lesley what are you doing here?" I asked.

The show was due to start so we arranged to have a chat during the interval, I rushed to the bathroom, and when I took my seat it was directly behind Lesley!

The planning of this could only have been guided by Spirit.

At two o'clock that afternoon I had decided to go to the theatre, and at the same time Lesley was in London with her sister, finalising arrangements for their father, who had to move home. (I had not even known she was in England).

It was Lesley's sister who had planned the show, saying they needed a break because they had been working very hard on their father's behalf. During the interval we rushed out, Lesley telephoned Nairobi to tell John, who was delighted we had met in this way.

Too many coincidences I think you will agree!

Getting Lesley and I to the same theatre on the same day, to have seats directly one behind the other was a feat in itself. I would not have been so surprised had it been Opera, which Lesley loved, but Motown would not have been her choice or mine, though it turned out to be wonderful and we danced to many of the songs.

I do often wonder WHEN the planning actually starts for such meetings, even going back to how we met and where, such a lot of plotting and dare I say manipulating? I only know it is very exciting indeed.

I keep saying that Spirit cannot possibly surprise me any-more, but they do and every time I say they cannot do anything more surprising!

Sadly, Lesley passed to Spirit in her mid 50's. I will always remember her beautiful smile, kind nature, true sense of fun and the kindness she showed to me on so many occasions.

I remain in contact with John, and am grateful to have been able to continue to visit his home.

During the writing of this book I have been constantly reminded of how Lesley so wanted to be part of it, and now she is, just not in the way she thought she would be.

I am grateful to her for encouraging me, and making me believe people would be interested in my many stories about the interaction between those in the Spirit world and those in the physical world.

...

COINCIDENCE OR SYNCHRONICITY?
SIMPLY SPIRIT GUIDING US.

In February 2006, I travelled to London to attend an appointment at the American Embassy, for a work visa to the U.S.A.

I decided to travel by train to enjoy a lovely journey through the English countryside, arriving safely in London in less than three hours. From Euston station I took a taxi to the Embassy in Grosvenor Square, arriving an hour early.

Fate was obviously on my side, because I was allowed into the building despite being very early for my appointment (the embassy staff are usually very strict about such things).

By four o'clock in the afternoon I was out again, so decided to get something to eat before catching my train home later. I walked towards Oxford Street, reflecting on the fact that Vern, an American friend in Spirit, had come to sit with me while I was waiting in the Embassy to be interviewed.

Vern was a policeman in Baton Rouge, Louisiana, who had passed to Spirit almost three years previously. I had spent Christmas with him, his wife Dianne and their family for what turned out to be the last Christmas I would spend with them all. I wasn't surprised that he came to accompany me as I made plans for my next trip to America, because I would be visiting his family, who he loved dearly.

On the corner of Oxford Street there was a shop selling luggage and handbags, and I felt compelled to go in, despite the fact that I already had far too many suitcases and bags! I wandered aimlessly around, still not sure what on earth I was doing in the shop, when my attention was drawn to the back. There on a table were Italian silk ties that were reduced in price, and, always one for a bargain, I looked through them.

One of the ties was a bright shade of blue and had 'English Bobbies' (policeman) printed all over it. I was reminded of the time that I'd taken an English police uniform as a gift to Vern some years previously, something he had always wanted. On impulse I bought the tie, knowing that Dianne would love to hear the story when I visited her and that Vern would have liked me to take her such a gift.

Happy with my purchase, I found a small café for a quick bite to eat, before looking for a black cab to take me back to Euston station. As always, there were many taxis lining the street, so I took the first empty one.

The driver was unusually chatty. He'd obviously recognised that my accent was from the North of England, and he mentioned that he'd known a lady who lived not far from the town where I was living at that time.

My mobile phone rang, interrupting our conversation. I answered it to a lady who was enquiring about tickets for an event I was organizing for the following Saturday. At the end of the week, it was to be my birthday and, instead of birthday presents, I'd asked all my personal friends to support the evening of Mediumship.

The event was a fundraiser for the Korogocho project in Nairobi, a project where those who are homeless, sick and dying were being helped by a Nun, and her helpers, to receive daily food, medication and a little love. I had asked the committee at a local church to allow me to use the church to do more fund-raising and planned an evening of 90 minutes of mediumship, followed by supper and a disco, all ending at midnight with all proceeds going to the fund.

Having heard the conversation, the taxi driver asked what I did. I explained that I was a medium. He quickly said that he didn't really believe in 'all that,' before saying, "But my dad was a faith healer. He used to go on the bus to give healing to people and never charged for it."

The taxi driver sounded very proud of his father, so we discussed healing and I thought it was just like Spirit to put him in my pathway. He even knew about Spiritualism's very own respected healer, Harry Edwards (now in Spirit), and obviously believed in the power of 'all that' healing, which made me smile.

By the time we arrived at Euston Station, he looked up at the meter, which registered almost £7. "See that?" he said, pointing at the meter. "Put that money in your fund on Saturday night for the children." I was so touched by his kindness that I shook his hand and asked his name. "David," he said. "And if my dad ever comes to talk to you, tell him I said 'hello!'"

David was typical of so many people who say they don't believe in life after death, but who often have a story to tell. I was very grateful to him and have many times told this particular story.

I had a little glow of happiness around me for the rest of the journey home because what had started as a long, stressful day had ended beautifully.
The following Saturday we were almost snowed in but fortunately, the event did go ahead. My aim and prediction had been to have 80 people there and to make £1000. Well, we did have 80 people there and made just over the £1000, David's contribution adding to the pot.

So, to all the David's out there I would say: doubt, if you must, but continue doing the good you are doing to help other people, and we will all benefit from your kindness. The people in Nairobi were certainly very grateful. There is a Kenyan saying "Many people doing small things are making a huge difference!"

...

SYNCHRONICITY AT IT'S BEST

Many years ago, I accompanied a medium and his wife to Clitheroe Spiritualist church, as we had planned to go out for a meal together afterwards. It's a tiny church and there were about thirty people congregated on that particular evening. During the course of the service, the medium gave a message to a lady sitting in the front row, nothing dramatic, just a normal sort of message.

Toward the end of the service, though, and during the last hymn, the lady became very agitated and began to cry. After the service came to a close, the medium went to speak to the lady and asked me over to have a word with her too, as a Minister because her daughter had died recently, so recently, in fact, that the funeral was yet to be held.

I sat with the lady, her daughter and young granddaughter, just chatting to them and offering my condolences, because, as I have said a thousand times, there is no greater loss than the loss of a child. During our chat, the daughter in Spirit talked to me and expressed something she would like to have happen at her funeral.

During the course of the next few years there were many changes in my life and changes at the Spiritualist church. I remember doing a sitting for the family once, and then seeing them again at a demonstration, but apart from that, we lost contact altogether.

Several years later, in 2017, I woke up one morning and just knew I had to go to Clitheroe, a town about 30 minutes from where I lived. I telephoned my friend Sheila and asked if she'd like to meet me there, which she was happy to do.

We had lunch and then, with just another half an hour before our time was up in the car park, Sheila suggested a last stop at a new shoe shop that had opened.

We walked in and immediately the young owner said, "Its Val, isn't it?"

I searched my memory and asked if she was the very young girl who had accompanied her mother and grandmother to the Clitheroe church, just after her aunt had died. She said she was and what followed was truly amazing.

The young girl said, "I can't believe this! Today is the date of my aunt's anniversary, and yesterday my gran lost her brother on her own birthday." She then telephoned her mother, so that we could have a chat and I asked her to pass on my best wishes to her gran.

The Spiritual timing of our 'chance' meetings really struck me afterwards. Firstly, I was allowed to be the medium to give a mother a brief message from her newly-passed daughter, which gave her and the sister of the deceased a lot of comfort.

Secondly and during our initial brief chat, the young woman in Spirit came to me and gave information about her forthcoming funeral, which brought reassurance and a little peace to her mother.

On another occasion the young woman gave true evidence of her life as it had been, during a public demonstration, and later during a private reading.

Finally, years later, I 'coincidentally' walk into a shop owned by her niece on the very day of the anniversary of her passing and on the day after which her grandmother had lost her brother!

We are never separated from people we have loved, even if they have passed to Spirit. Everything that happened for this family, through me as the medium, proved this universal truth, bringing a lot of comfort to them.

I feel sure there was enough evidence to show that a young woman was alive and well in Spirit, and close by. She had chosen the medium she was willing to speak to, subsequently leading that same medium to where she needed her to be at a very significant time, when her mother needed reassurance yet again.

If you're still waiting for evidence from your loved ones, talk to them, ask them to choose their medium and then lead you to that particular medium. I hope there will come a time when you will have just such a synchronistic meeting.

I do not believe that chance or coincidences are part of the equation. I have learned during the past forty years of communicating with Spirit that there is no such thing as coincidence. Spirit intervention determines that you will notice signs, symbols, coincidences for what they really are, clearly the close presence of Spirit manifesting in your life.

Very recently I gave a message to someone whose response was "I've waited fifty years for that message from my loved one." Mediums will never be in charge of when a communication is to take place, but if we let ourselves be led, we may be allowed to give wonderfully evidential communication to those who are grieving the loss of their loved ones.

...

PERFECT TIMING

Linda was a lady from Pennsylvania, U.S.A who I first met in England during a seminar organized by the internationally known medium, Don Galloway. We quickly became friends, after she had a reading with me. She invited me to stay with her, the initial visit becoming an annual tradition.

Linda's elderly Mum had chosen to move to a wonderful facility for the elderly. Her health had been deteriorating for a few years. When I initially visited, we would take her out for an ice-cream sundae (to a favourite place called 'Friendly's') but in time we had to take the ice-cream sundae to her. One year when I was visiting, Linda's mother wasn't well at all. Linda, being a very good daughter visited as often as she could.

Every day for a month Linda's mother was coming to the end of her life and, on the night before I was leaving, I went to bed, and was dropping off to sleep, when my Voice said, 'This is the end, this is the last stage. At four o'clock in the morning, she will die, but before she dies, this is what will happen to her....'

I cannot remember all of the details now, but my Voice explained a staged process that would help to reassure my friend Linda. Her mother was prepared to go and they would lead her gently to the Spirit World, where her beloved husband, who adored her as only a Jewish husband can adore his wife, would be waiting. At seven o'clock in the morning there was a knock on the door. Linda said, "I'm sorry to disturb you." I interjected, "Before you say anything more, has your Mum passed?" she replied, "Yes. At four o'clock in the morning." I said, "Come and sit down here and I'll tell you what Spirit told me last night, before you discuss it with anyone else.

Linda said she'd share the information with her brothers, who had been with their mother and who didn't see any sense in disturbing her sleep. They told Linda not to worry. She had done as much as she could for their mother while she was alive.

It had been very stressful looking after her, as mom had become quite difficult, as often happens when people succumb to old age and illness. When Linda checked with her brothers, everything had happened just as Spirit had told me it would. They were equally relieved to know that the passing was peaceful, and that her beloved husband, their father, would be there waiting for her.

I know that the information given to Linda helped her tremendously. Our connection to one another was almost accidental. Linda would never have said she was a Spiritualist. She attended events to kindly escort a disabled friend to England. When her husband died suddenly in a car crash, she had a sitting with Don Galloway, but didn't really see any other mediums. Then she met me and I gave her evidence from her husband during the sitting, and that's why she invited me over.

I will always be grateful to her for her kindness, which I was able to repay thanks to the love of Spirit. Spirit gave me information to help those who were left behind. In this case, it was Linda and her brothers. Often, we are put in each other's paths, because of the support our friendship can bring at special times, which we wouldn't expect we'd share when we first met. I'm happy that I could be there for Linda, and I'm always happy to help anyone who feels 'left behind' by a loved one. In truth, though, they never leave us, they simply leave behind the physical body and continue their eternal journey, making contact through mediums when they feel it is the right time to do so.

LEAVE IT TO SPIRIT.

On the 16th March, some years ago, I took the Sunday Service at Blackburn Spiritualist church. During the service, a contact was accepted by a friend, who was also a working medium.

I had never before given her a contact from her father, but on this occasion he spoke of 'someone in the family who was ill and whose illness had been misdiagnosed ', saying 'it was a blockage.'

My friend told me afterwards that he was referring to her sister, who had recently been admitted to hospital. I had no knowledge of this situation previously, as I had only returned the night before from a two-week working visit to Denmark.

On the Wednesday night of that same week, I was due to work in Morecambe. During the afternoon, I called in at the petrol station en-route and whilst I was there, I noticed that there were a few answer- phone messages on my mobile phone.

I dialled 123 to retrieve the messages, expecting the usual answer machine voice, but for some unexpected reason my friend (whom I'd passed on the message from her father to) answered! We were both surprised. I was surprised, because it was her voice rather than the usual recorded messages. She was surprised, because I had connected to her when she needed a friend, as her sister had just passed to Spirit. I couldn't help but feel that Spirit must have been at work, connecting us to one another. She explained that she was on her way to the Lancaster Royal Infirmary to meet the rest of her family there.

The following day she telephoned to ask me if I would officiate at the funeral service at the local crematorium. I was quite surprised by this request, simply because the whole family was Catholic. Nevertheless, I was honoured and agreed to do it.

I arranged to meet the family and duly presented myself to them. Everyone was there except for one sister, who had been travelling back from Australia for the funeral at the time. They were all reminiscing and sharing stories, and it was heart-warming to hear the happy memories flooding back in.

They laughed about their sister's terrible singing voice, and mentioned one song in particular, 'Toora Loora Loora', known as the Irish lullaby. I could barely say it, let alone sing it, but because this was such a special memory for the whole family (and especially so for the daughter of the sister who'd passed) they decided to try to find a CD of the music.

A few days went by, but they couldn't find it anywhere. (It was before the internet had made music readily available for download - we were not as advanced in those days!) The only course of action I could think of was to make an appeal to Spirit to help me to find it, which I did immediately.

The following day, I was due to work at Crewe Spiritualist church, but I had not received a confirmation of the booking so I telephoned the booking secretary, only to be told that I must have written the wrong date in my diary. This has rarely happened, if ever. I had already made arrangements to stay with a friend in a nearby Cheshire town so I visited him anyway.

Whilst I was there, I asked him if he knew where I could buy a CD of old-fashioned Irish music. He said that there were two Irishmen who sold CD's at the local Sandbach market, and that it might be worth checking out their stall. We picked up another friend en- route. On the journey to Sandbach, a Spirit Voice told me I would find the CD I was looking for in the third box.

We arrived at the market and very quickly realised that the Irish men were not even there. I couldn't believe it, since I'd just been told that I would find the CD there! After walking around for a little while, though, I spotted a stall selling CDs.

I started looking through the Irish music ones, but the stall owner insisted that he didn't have 'Toora Loora Loora.' He did offer to order it for the end of the week, though. "Too late!" I said, "I'll need it before then."

Just then, my friend came along side me and said with a smile, "Did you say "Toora, Loora, Loora?" I was thrilled - he had found it! When I looked down at the box, I realised that it wasn't the third box from the left, which I had been looking through, but the third box from the right! Spirit had been right again! I guarded the CD very well all the way home!

Friday arrived, and I took the funeral service at the crematorium. All of the sisters were sitting together in the front row, and their children were in the row behind them. When it came to telling the story of their special CD, I explained that I'd asked God for a sign that their sister had been received and that she was well. For her daughter, the music CD was just that sign.

The family were very emotional during the funeral service, but once the lullaby began to play, all of the sisters started singing and swaying in unison, the whole atmosphere changing from deep sadness to a celebration of their loved one's life.

Afterwards, there were many compliments about the service, but I know the story of how I came upon the CD will stick in the minds of everyone who attended and, hopefully, give them something to think about. There is truth in every religion but I believe that Spiritualism is the only religion that substantiates the fact that the soul lives on and is able to communicate with our physical world. Our Spirit loved ones prove that the love we had for each other will never die, which is often the emotional closure people need to feel. One of the sisters stopped me as I was leaving to go home and said, "You have put our Catholic services to shame. I'd like you to do my funeral!" Her words made me smile. I felt so grateful, in that moment, to be a Spiritualist Minister, bringing joy to the loved ones who must remain in the physical world, who often feel they have lost their nearest and dearest. We always try to make our services a celebration of life, something I know our loved ones in Spirit wish us to do.

...

WHEN THE SNOW THAWS
My first visit to a Spiritualist church was on the advice of a psychic in Fleetwood. I had asked her where my cousin was. She had been murdered as a teenager. The psychic said she is wandering around in the Spirit world! I really felt the need to do something, but had no idea what to do, to help her. She told me to go into a church to pray for her.

When I had been told my cousin had died "my voice" told me who had killed her. I know now that my mediumship was developing all through my childhood. It was not very nice to have such things said in my head, as it made me always feel I was a bad person.

I had always had what I call the "knowing" which means that when my voice tells me to take note of something I always have to know, for myself, if it is true. I have argued with this voice so many times, always to find out he is right in the end. I could have saved myself a lot of heartache had I listened.

My cousin had been a thin, frail little girl who was abused by her father from the age of 9 and subsequently had a baby to him around the age of 13. I was a couple of years younger than her and so did not know any of this when I was a child. When she was found in the water having been strangled, I believe she was 18 and I was 16.

My relationship with my mother had never been good unfortunately, and after my cousin died, I felt constantly guilty because when I was 14 my mother had asked if my cousin could come to live with us (she had never, ever asked my opinion about anything) I did not think it was a good idea. Maybe if I had known how she was being abused I might have made a different decision.

23

So, guilt, sadness etc., started my search, this leading me to the Spiritualist church and the rest, as they say, is history. 40 years later my life has never been better, thanks to Spirit.

As I have said before I had no knowledge of Spiritualism, or Spiritualist churches and was very surprised when I was 34, to discover that my family on my mother's side were Spiritualists, and that Grandmother and great grandmother were mediums.

Apparently, after my cousin died my grandmother and my cousin's parents came to visit us. They all went to Fleetwood Spiritualist church one evening.

Over 15 years later I went to have a sitting with a local psychic and when I asked questions about my cousin she said "but you have always known who killed her" I was totally shocked. Furthermore, she said "you went to their home and in the corner, there was a shrine to her" plus other things I prefer not to mention.

I so knew this to be right that I went directly to my mothers' shop and asked her if what I had always known to be true was something she had known. Her response was weird "Valerie, the snow is thawing". I asked if she had heard what I said and she told me the most incredible story. On the evening she had gone with her relatives to the church a male medium I know now to be the amazing Albert Best was in the middle of giving someone a message when he suddenly turned to my mother, pointed at her and said "you cannot get the answer to your question now – you will get it when the snow thaws"

We were both in shock and then I realized that the snow was starting to thaw and we could hear it plopping down the drain.

Later that year I went to my grandmother, who was 84, and

asked if she knew that her son had killed his own daughter, to which she replied "Valerie, I have always known".
I have only seen my cousin, in Spirit, once. After my grandmother died, I saw clairvoyantly, my great-grandmother, grandmother and my cousin. I thought that my grandmother could finally be at peace.

(I have chosen not to use names or personal details because there are still members of my cousin's family living and though I have no contact with them they have suffered enough.

My own childhood was not easy, born to parents who never seemed to speak to each other, such a strange atmosphere in the house. The only conversations I do remember were when my mother was telling my father that I was not doing things properly. From the age of 8 I cleaned house, did the shopping and looked after my sister who was 5 years younger. Always a clever girl, apparently, I eventually went to the grammar school. Never, once, do I remember my parents telling me I had done something right, only the contrary.

For that reason, I am indebted to Spirit for rescuing me. After a very unhappy childhood I fell into a marriage with a man who suffered mental illness and was paranoid. It took me 20 years to leave the relationship because I had promised myself I would stay until my son was grown up, which I did.

Hearing stories like my cousin's and knowing what a terrible life she had certainly helped me to get my life into a different perspective —and also has helped me to appreciate the healing power of the knowledge Spirit have given to me. This in turn has given me a compassion for people who are genuinely hurting and an empathy with anyone who has been restricted, unloved or held back for any reason.

When people tell me their sad stories they often say "Oh, you wouldn't understand" but in most cases I can absolutely understand. I am grateful never to have suffered the physical loss of a child, but many other aspects of pain, sadness and isolation I have experienced. I do, however, have the sadness of not having seen my son for almost 30 years, a different sort of loss, but I do know I could have been a better mother under different circumstances. In the 1970's there were no women's refuges, no social security to help financially, Thankfully, that has been rectified now, so no-one, man or woman, needs to stay in a toxic relationship.

These days I am just happy to be able to celebrate so many years of personal freedom and to have had the opportunity to reach out to so many people who Spirit have led me to in the hope of them finding ease for their pain, no matter if the pain is mental, emotional, or physical.

I have appreciated the true value of the healing power of the Spirit communications, having been allowed to give and receive messages of comfort. This has encouraged me to know that those in the Spirit world really do know better than we do what we need, which is not quite the same as what we want.

Thank to Spirit I feel content, and I will always remember the words of my voice "Remember you are who you are, not despite everything, but because of it."
Whenever you feel the world is against you please take these words on board. They healed me and I am sure they will heal you when you need them the most.

...

CHILDREN IN SPIRIT
LUKAS
I have often wondered how long it takes Spirit to plan for people to meet each other, which is often to allow Spirit people to communicate with loved ones who are still in the physical world. Marianne and I met at Stansted Hall, a beautiful house in the countryside in Essex, which houses the world-renowned Arthur Findlay College. Marianne is a

Swiss lady who came as a student each year, then one year she chose to come on my course. A couple of years later she asked would I go over to Bern and do a few little workshops, not big ones, just little ones to allow the students to have truly concentrated teaching. She wanted to get sincere people together, so I did go, thoroughly enjoying the Swiss people who came.

I was invited to her sister's home for dinner and this was where I met her mother, a strong feisty little women, a lady who wouldn't do anything that the nurses and the doctors told her, told lies about her legs when they needed bandaging, and who said she could manage them herself which she couldn't, quite typical of people of her generation who had to learn to be fiercely independent.

Over the years I became very involved with Marianne's small family, with her sister and brother in law and their two children.   They became my Swiss family. I remember my first visit to their house in the Emmental. Everyone was talking Swiss German, so I wandered around the living room. I noticed an encaustic wax picture on the wall and for no reason I said 'Oh that looks just like Star Wars!' (I've never even seen Star Wars movies!) Suddenly this little boy of nine grabbed my hand, ran me up the stairs into his huge bedroom where everything was Star Wars, Star Wars Lego, posters of Star Wars. He was very excited so I just sat there, listening to him chattering away. He had no English and I just smiled to myself, thinking 'I've never seen a Star Wars film'. I loved this child from that moment and when I went to Canada a few weeks later I bought him a Lego Star Wars watch with a Darth Vader figure on, as well as buying something for his sister who is two years older than him, a brother and sister who loved each other very much, and shared a lot of quality time with each other.

I clearly remember that, on that first visit, as we sat at the dinner table he suddenly turned to me and "don't worry, be happy". His mother, who speaks very good English, asked how he knew to say that and he just smiled.

In time he could speak English and we had some very nice conversations. Lukas was truly a very sensitive boy, and as often happens with teenagers when he was 13 he became moody and a little difficult. Don't worry I said, he'll get over it and come out the other side OK. Never have I regretted saying anything so much.

A few weeks later I received a text from Marianne simply saying that Lukas had shot himself. I telephoned immediately, hoping I had misread something.
When she confirmed that Lukas had indeed taken his own life I just couldn't believe it. I felt as if something was twisting a knife in my heart. He was a gentle, kind, Piscean boy who had so much to live for, parents and a sister who loved him as did everyone in his family.

I asked when did it happen, and where? Apparently he'd come home from school that day and had phoned the Police, simply saying 'I've got my Grandfather's gun and I'm going to kill myself and in the next ten minutes you need to come to the house and find my body because I don't want my sister to find me' and then he did what he told them he would do, in his bedroom.

It was very, very hard for everyone to believe, and in the midst of it all, his grandmother was ill and other older members of the family were ill, a dreadful time for the whole family.

The day after he died I remember driving, tears pouring down my face. My Voice said Lukas was being bullied at school so I emailed Marianne straight away and she got in touch with the Police. They went to the school to check and it was true! He was being bullied because he was protecting younger children. I was also told there were three boys responsible, one being much shorter than the other two. Everything my Voice told me was true.

It transpired that every day they were taking money from

him. He was saving up to be a Gunsmith and they had had all his money. I can only hope the fact that I was given true information from Spirit helped his loving family. Shortly after that I sent thoughts to him, asking him to give me messages for his family, but there was no communication from him at all.

About 3 or 4 months later Marianne emailed me and said 'Mum is pretty much on her way out, they're expecting her to die any day and you're due to come over so we have to wait and see when you get here how things are'.

(I hadn't been able to go to Lukas' funeral because my friend Joyce had come to stay for her annual visit. She developed gall bladder problems and was in Blackburn hospital for two weeks which meant I couldn't even go to the funeral in Switzerland. As soon as I was able to, I booked a flight, just a gesture to show I was supporting this lovely family.)

As soon as I arrived in Switzerland Marianne told me that someone from the hospital would phone to say what time in the night her mum had died. It was Friday night and her mum, Rosemary, was very comfortable. She had had no drink, no food and no heart medication since Wednesday so it would be a quiet, natural process and she would just die peacefully sometime in the night.

The following morning no-one from the hospital had called, so we went to the hospital. Rosemary was lying in the bed with her eyes closed. She looked very peaceful, very dry around the mouth. I walked into the room and I put my hands through the little bars of the bed. Rosemary grabbed my hand as if she would never let go, so I told Marianne, 'I'll just sit quietly and give her some healing for whatever it is her soul needs'.

Marianne was very attentive, she kept coming to her, and each time her mum threw her arms out, as if to push Marianne away. On previous visits Marianne and her sister had gently told their mum to go to Lukas, saying that he would be waiting for her.

After a while she calmed so Marianne put cream on her face and moistened her lips, but she just still clung on to my hand. After about an hour and a half we thought we'd better leave as we couldn't do any more at that stage. We were due to visit Lukas' mum, dad and sister. We drove up the mountain to where Lukas had lived with his Mum and Dad, as we were to have dinner, and still nothing from Lukas, not a word, though I had felt his energy around me.

They were doing a barbeque, and suddenly at 5.55pm I said to Marianne. 'Quick, go and ring up the hospital now.' She rushed to the phone and I assumed her Mum had died.

When she came back she had a weird look on her face so I asked her 'What's the matter? Has she gone?' and she said 'No! She's just woken up and said she's hungry and thirsty and demanded a yoghurt and something to drink' I asked what the nurses did and she told us they had given her a yoghurt and she had eaten half of it! We were all in shock.

The following morning Marianne telephoned the hospital and they said 'Your mother has just demanded that we get her out of the bed and take her to the window, to make sure she's still in Bern'. Of course, they did exactly that, then she ate something and had some water. The day after that she said to them 'Now you can put me in an elderly home and don't tell my daughters, they've been trying to kill me you know.' (That is how she interpreted their gentle encouragement for her to go peacefully)

The doctor said it was not possible that she had survived because she had had no heart medication, not one drop of water, she'd had no food since Wednesday and this was Saturday.

Rosemary came out of the hospital and my last photo of her is of her wearing a shocking pink cardigan. On the photo she's eating the champagne truffles I took over for her, never thinking she would be able to eat them. She did die some weeks later but totally at peace. She asked her girls to come to see her at the home and said she was at peace and ready to go to Spirit. She wanted them to take care of each other. She told them she had seen Lukas and she had seen her husband so she knew she was going to be alright. She did die shortly after this, very peacefully.

My next visit over to Switzerland had been booked 18 months ahead as always. Marianne said she wanted us to go and look at Lukas's grave. The family had put up a headstone and they'd been working on the little garden on the grave.

I agreed, so we went to buy something for the grave and on the drive up to his home Lukas spoke to me. He said 'As it's my birthday I would like to do a sitting with you as my Mum's gift from me'. Of course I did so willingly!

His mum cried a lot, which was a great release for her. It was just absolutely beautiful, Lukas saying all the things he wanted to say to put the record straight so that she and the family would not have any guilt and I believe this brought peace to her.

The following weekend she came to a workshop that I was holding and she brought with her some photos of Lukas and Lukas and his sister together. At 1 o'clock she became very agitated and started crying and she said 'Lukas is here and I don't know what to do"

I'd already suggested to Marianne that perhaps we could get people to link in with the photos using their mediumship but I had thought it was too soon for Sonja. Although she was quite agitated I asked her if she would like me to ask the students, without them knowing that he was her son, to look at the photos and see what evidence or information they received from them, in the hope that they could actually link in with Lukas.

She said she would like that so they did so and the information that came out about his real personality, his real nature, games he played, as well as very personal private things, known only to his family. Some of the little things his Mum had said and things about his Dad were all very relevant. Lukas' Mum and Dad each have a motorbike and they were going to teach Lukas to ride as well. All those special little pieces of evidence helped to change her energy, and gave her a lot of information to share with her husband and daughter.

I remember saying to his sister, a very clever girl who has written stories and done illustrations for years. 'You know you're very clever at writing and illustrating books, maybe one day you could do one which could be given to every school child about how to protect themselves'.

I felt sure it was important to the family to know that his death should have meaning. As a Spiritualist I know everything is in its right order, that we die when we are meant to and in time we realise why but not everyone has this knowledge, and it will always be difficult for any parent to understand why their child must die before them.

Lukas had been very brave, wanting to protect his sister and the saddest thing is that he left a note saying 'The world will now be a better place because there's one less worthless idiot in it', such is the power of bullies!

Lukas was just so kind and so sweet, it really was very, very sad but I have wondered so many times when Spirit decided that Marianne and I would meet. I have no doubt, whatsoever, that we were meant to meet.

Lukas' parents have written to me, saying I am part of their family and the loss of Lukas would have been so much harder to get through without my support. I will always be grateful to be able to give it to them.

They actually came to the Lindum Hotel at Christmas (somewhere that has become my Spiritual home) because they didn't want to be at home without Lukas. We had a good time together, we talked about Lukas quite a lot, and for these parents, who had loved and lost their beautiful boy, there are good times and then there are very, very sad times. I believe parents will always think that their child should be with them, but at least it's reassuring to think now that they've got a real insight because they've had evidence that their son is safe in Spirit, and now they know he is helping children in our world who are being bullied.

Miriam, his sister, sadly lost three relatives in about 6 months, two grand-parents and her brother, very hard at 16 but the evidence has shown that they are together so we're waiting for more. Lukas came through twice recently at Stansted and once again I was able to pass on messages to his family.

Nothing will ever replace him but I hope the messages he has brought have proven to his loved ones that they WILL meet again.

To every parent who has ever lost a child I would simply say : send your thoughts to your child, and they will continue to feel your love.

I read once that "you can never lose someone as long as you hold them in your heart", just words I know but sometimes that is all there is, plus the memories that are as real today as they ever were.

...

THE TORTOISESHELL BUTTERFLY
During the many years I have worked with, and for, the Spirit world I have experienced many occasions where butterflies have manifested, sometimes in the strangest of circumstances.
One of the most beautiful experiences was during the summer of 2005.

I had received a telephone call earlier that year from a man called David, who said he had been recommended to call me by a mutual friend called Gwen, who lost her son when he was just a young boy.

David asked when I was to be in the South of England and I told him I would be there at the beginning of July, as I would be staying with my friend Jeanne after I had worked at Brighton church for their long weekend. We arranged a suitable time for him to come for a sitting and I said I looked forward to meeting him.

On June 25th Jeanne came to Blackburn to take part in a fund-raising day I had arranged. Unfortunately, during the day she fell, broke her hip and was rushed to the Blackburn hospital where she later had an operation.
Naturally, this meant that I would not, after all, be staying with her the following week.

I telephoned David, to tell him I was sorry but the sitting could not go ahead as arranged. He was quite insistent that he needed, and wanted, to have a sitting so I checked my diary and said I could not see when it would be possible.

He persisted, asking that if there was any way it could be possible would I let him know. After checking again, I found only one hour was available during the whole year and that was when I was due to work on Manchester week at the Arthur Findlay College. I telephoned him and he agreed to come during that week so, again, all seemed well.
I did not know at that time why I felt it was so important for him to have a sitting.

On the day of the appointment he arrived with his second wife. I went to the bathroom before doing the sitting, and I heard my voice say "he lost his boy". I rushed into the Blue room, where the sitting was to take place, and asked if it was true that he had lost his son, to which he replied "yes I have"

The boy kept saying 17 to me so I asked his dad if he was seventeen when he died. No, said his dad but the boy kept repeating it. I asked how long ago he had died and he said 6 years. I then asked how old his son had been when he died and he said 11, so of course he was letting me know his present age.

I felt a terrible pain in my head, dizziness and disorientation, which I assumed to be his son's condition. He said he understood. There followed much that is typical during an evidential sitting, memories, dates and situations to validate the information.

What happened next was not typical. David, his wife and I heard a sound. I pointed to the butterfly that was inside the room and flapping against the window, saying I thought Russell, Gwen's son must be here as he often manifested a Red Admiral butterfly, but David said that now he knew his son truly was communicating because it was actually a tortoiseshell butterfly, which his son manifested when he was giving evidence to someone.

At this point the butterfly flew directly to David, landing on his nose and staying there for about 3 seconds, 3 absolutely breath-taking seconds! I told David his son was giving him a kiss! I felt it he said, tears of happiness streaming down his face. I cried and his wife also cried. As I concluded the sitting David said "that was the best sitting I ever had". We were all overwhelmed by the appearance of the butterfly and even more overwhelmed by the feeling of love in the room. If any of us had doubted before that the love of Spirit could manifest, we could doubt it no more. David then explained that his son had had a brain tumour, hence the physical feelings I had had but we were left in no doubt whatsoever that the personality of a young boy of amazing courage had survived death.

As mediums we have momentary connection to our sitters and yet at the same time we feel so connected to the family unit and it is my eternal gratitude to Spirit that I was allowed to be part of that particular sitting.

As a child I was told never to touch a butterfly or it would die, and yet here in that moment a butterfly touched a man with pure love and I witnessed it.

Afterwards, I thought how wonderful to have been able to have taken a photo, but when you are caught in the moment you cannot possibly think, and maybe you are not meant to because we get so caught up in technology sometimes we may actually miss a precious moment, and there is nothing more beautiful than feeling, once more, the love of Spirit.

DAVID'S LETTER TO ME, 27th September 2005

Dear Val,
Sorry for the delay in writing to you, it's been rather a hectic summer! Many thanks for an amazing reading in July at Stansted, which still now makes me smile and gives me a warm glow.

This is the first reading, of many I have had, which felt as if I was actually having a conversation with my son. You knew immediately that I had a son in Spirit and that he had something wrong with his head and a vision problem. You were correct in saying that he passed 6 years ago and that he would be 17 now and gave me so much evidence it was staggering. But for me it was the conversation which was remarkable, and just like ones we used to have, but this time he was giving me valuable advice on how to deal with life and the rest of the family.

A butterfly had entered the room early in the reading and was flying around the window. You mentioned that you knew that my son had met Russell Byrne (a mutual friend's son in Spirit) and that Russell often used butterflies in communication. My son was a nature lover and his favourite butterfly was a tortoiseshell, at an emotional part of the reading the butterfly, a tortoiseshell, circled my head and then landed on my nose, a kiss from my son! This was certainly the most memorable part of the reading of which I will be eternally grateful to you for the wonderful and 100% accurate communication. I hope this will be suitable to put into your next book, if you need any more information please let us know.

We know you are a busy lady, but if your work brings you to Sussex again, we'd love to meet you again in a professional or social capacity. We hope soon to set up workshops and it would be wonderful if we could book you for some in the future.

With kindest wishes and thanks again,
Yours sincerely,
David McCarthy.

So, here we were 13 years later, June 2018. I was invited to visit a Spiritual organization in Maidstone, Kent, for the first time. It was a lovely warm evening and there were not many people there, but they were a lovely welcoming group who meet in a community centre.

Sometimes mediums complain that there are not more people in the audience. It is more sensible to wonder why we are placed where we are to do our work.

During the course of my Demonstration of Mediumship, I gave a message to a man, whose wife helped him to understand or remember some things.

After the service finished, he came to me and said "Do you remember the butterfly at Stansted Hall?" I was very shocked as that particular incident had been many years previously and I had not seen the couple since that time, but the sitting itself is indelibly imprinted on my mind, something I could never forget.

If anyone doubts that Spirit make the appointment, and

choose the medium they want I hope this story will make them think differently. Spirit people are intelligent and know what they want, who they want and when to bring an appointment about, of that I have no doubt whatsoever, and I believe this story validates my thinking.

...

PSYCHOMETRY WHEN USED BY A MEDIUM
I have done readings, from flowers as well as articles, since I first started developing my mediumship and have just assumed that everyone understood what the word psychometry meant. To help everyone to understand the following story I just want to take a few minutes to explain what it actually means to psychometrise an article.

The word Psychometry actually means to trace the origin of an article so, for example, if someone asked for a table to be psychometrised it should be possible to trace the origin of the tree, and where it grew, that produced the final article – the table.

Apparently, I have always had this ability as one of my natural gifts, people used to hand me articles and I would give accurate information about their current lives and circumstances. No matter what the article was I could give information about it, though I had no idea what I was doing. I have given information from froth on beer glasses, personal items of clothing, jewellery, personal artefacts etc.

Sometimes the police use people who are very good at this type of psychic work to help them to find people who are missing, or to solve cases they are struggling with.

At first, I thought it was just some sort of game, but I soon realised there could be a very serious aspect of this particular gift. A psychic or medium can "read" the energy of the sitter by holding an article belonging to them. Just shaking hands with someone can start the process.

In the late 1980's I was in Belgium. My host asked me to

psychometrise a stone, just an ordinary looking stone. I held it for a minute or two and then described a mountain and an area that looked like a desert. It was certainly a very dusty area. My host, who asked me to "feel the energy" of the stone said he had just flown back from such an area abroad and that he had picked it up just before he left.

I continued to do psychometry on a regular basis, until I realized that I could tune in quickly to the Spirit world via this means, so in my early days of working I always asked the sitter if I could hold a watch, ring or other personal item.

I had had readings from other "mediums, who used to ask for an article of mine, never understanding that unless the information became evidence of a spirit person, by establishing the personality, then it was simply information, not Spirit communication.

 Most of the people who read cards for other people are mainly using their ability to "read" the energy when the cards have been shuffled by the recipient
I came to understand that every article holds the energy of the owner and that flowers, when in someone's home, hold the energy of the person or people in the home.

I was asked to do flower readings for people, during which someone gave me a flower and I gave a message from it , many times finding that Spirit loved ones came clearly and evidentially.

As my mediumship progressed I began to do flower demonstrations at Spiritualist churches, again a means of giving messages of information of the recipients' life circumstances and also it brought Spirit people closer to me.

In time I learnt that in the hands of a psychic, only information known to the recipient was given, whereas in the hands of a medium, having the ability to receive communication from the Spirit world, pure evidence established proof to the recipients that their loved ones really were communicating.

In recent times the law regarding Psychics and Mediums has changed and it is no longer allowed to give information about the future whilst holding an article of any sort, flowers included. This is simply because it is classed, by law, as fortune telling, which is illegal in the United Kingdom.

Hopefully, understanding the workings of psychometry will help you to enjoy the following story, and appreciate the intricacies involved in giving messages, using an article without knowing to whom the article belongs, or having any information about it whatsoever.

...

BODY FOUND IN PINIE TREES IN THE FOREST
I worked for a Spiritualist church in Ontario for about 15 years, teaching at workshops, doing public demonstrations of Mediumship, training people for trance, and taking church services. One of my favourite evenings of mediumship was when I did a flower service.

Natural mediums can usually just give psychic information and/or mediumistic evidence when handed a flower, having had no instruction on how to do it.

The trained medium was taught to "read" the flower by taking notice of the petals, the condition of the flower, the straightness or otherwise of the stem to lead them to giving information, and possible evidence from Spirit as well.

In years gone by some mediums specialised in doing flower services, asking that the people who attended each brought a flower with them, preferably from their own garden, or which they had had in their home for some time. The natural medium simply allows Spirit to inspire them, initially connecting with the vibrations of the person who had brought them, or simply using their mediumship, giving any

information given to them by the Spirit communicator.
To respect the latest laws governing mediumship in the UK,
I explain before even touching a flower that as soon as I get
a contact from the Spirit world I must put the flower down,
and concentrate on the Spirit contact.

The reason for this is simple for those who don't know.
Should there be any information given about the future, of
course a flower cannot predict, but if a medium is linking
with a person from Spirit world, the Spirit person may give
information about a future event, a totally different thing.

Luckily, I was a natural from the first time I touched a flower
during my first ever flower workshop, and shortly after I
started doing them a little girl, from Spirit, appointed
herself my "guide" for this particular aspect of mediumship.
Each time now before I start I see this little girl and she
simply tells me everything. Consequently there have been
some absolutely amazing pieces of information and
evidence.

If I had taken notes over the years I could probably have
written a book just about this, but a recent flower service
stands out in my mind.

As always I arrived early so I could hide away in the office,
as I never want to see who brings the flowers in. On
entering the church each person was given a cup and a
number unique to them and their flower.

Here is how it works for me: Once everyone is seated the
chairperson brings me into the church. After saying a
prayer, I give a brief explanation of what they may expect,
saying that I do not want to know whose flower I am
working with until I ask for this. I give the number, give
whatever information I am told to give and when I feel it to
be appropriate because I have a connection with Spirit I ask
whose flower it is. As soon as I am connecting knowingly
with the recipient I hand their flower to a chairperson who
puts it into a vase of water.

On this particularly memorable evening I seemed to have quite a few people saying "no" to me which I am not used to during flower services, and then towards the end I picked up a huge piece of a branch from a pine tree. Holding it up I jokingly said "who has brought a Christmas tree without putting baubles on it", then I started giving the evidence I was being given. Unusually I did not hand the branch to the chairperson but laid it down and kept making stroking movements above it. The first communicator from Spirit was an older man who planted trees and gave evidence I don't now remember, then suddenly I was aware of a younger man and instinctively knew it was the son of the lady I was connecting to, but I didn't say so.

I described a forest in quite some detail and gave whatever information the young man wanted me to and I believe I closed the service shortly after this.
I was tired and quite stressed due to the number of "no's" I had received, so after the service I sat at the back waiting for my friend to drive me home. It is difficult to express how sometimes our emotion becomes involved in the process, but it is simply in my case because I feel I AM the Spirit person when I am working.

As I was waiting, one of the two ladies who accepted the message from the pine branch asked if she could explain to me what it had all meant. Still feeling frustrated, but not wishing to be rude I agreed and what she said totally shocked me.

She said that the young man was her son, the original communicator who planted the trees having been her dad. Her son had been missing for four years and had only recently been found, in a forest with his physical remains nestled in pine needles!

She was so grateful for the contact from him, and gave me a beautiful bookmark she had had made with his picture on. It is hard to imagine what any parent goes through when they lose a child, but to lose a child and not be able to see the body or say goodbye is doubly distressing.

At least now he had been found she could begin her natural grieving process, the Spirit contact via my mediumship telling her he was now safe.

So, in a short space of time this mother and her family had found her son again, physically, and now she could leave the church knowing that he was safe in Spirit with family and loved ones.

As is so often the case this message was her son phoning home to say he was safe, truly the blessing of mediumship. I have since checked on the internet and saw that this lovely young man was truly a dare-devil, always pushing himself more and more, because he wanted to be out in nature in extreme circumstances. I can only hope his family gained comfort from knowing he died in an environment he loved so much.

...

A young woman, attending a Spiritualist church service for the first time had a life-changing experience during this event. Here is the story in her own words:

CINDY'S STORY
In the spring of 2017, my dear friend, Vicky, was diagnosed with cancer. She "did it all" as a mom of two sons, advocating constantly for her son, Hayden, especially, as he progressed through elementary school managing his CP condition.

She was "large and in charge," a force of positivity, generosity, and Super Mom in our school community, even in the midst of aggressive cancer treatments. By the fall of 2017, she was working through an incredible Bucket List and had every detail of her own funeral planned, including asking me to sing Hallelujah at her Celebration of Life. The venue, songs, readings, eulogies and which tiara she would wear to meet her Maker were all in her control.

It was my great honour to have the opportunity to share my rewritten version of Hallelujah with her prior to her passing on Mother's Day, 2018. As far as I'm concerned, she even somehow orchestrated the significant date of her passing. When I saw her brother's name come up on my phone that bright, sunny Mother's Day morning, even before I answered the call, I actually laughed and said out loud, "Nailed it!!!!"

Fast forward to the following Saturday, her Celebration of Life at a local park community room venue was packed, her tiara front and centre adorning her urn and the Hallelujah captured her essence perfectly. I was among the last to leave after cleaning up and her husband, Dave, INSISTED I take home one of the two, large, mainly pink rose bouquets.

A couple days later my friend, Pat, told me about Val, the visiting medium from England she was hosting in her home. There was to be a "flower reading service" that Wednesday at the First Spiritualist Church. She asked if I would like to attend the service. Thinking of the gorgeous roses in my home, and of Vicky, I eagerly reserved my spot. I held that perfect pink rose all day at school and went to the Flower Service, taking a seat way in the back row.

With everything in me, I maintained a 'poker face' when Val FINALLY got to my rose, Vicky's rose. She had picked up the other flowers and handled them throughout whole readings. When she picked up my flower, she immediately said, "Oh this flower is very delicate. This person has recently passed to Spirit. I have to be very gentle with this flower." She then laid the rose on the podium as gently as you would handle a baby bird with a broken wing. She spoke of Vicky's neck pain, of her drug haze, of Sept. 4th, and of the location of a visitor sitting to her right touching her hair. All true!

44

In the end, Vicky's "stoner" texts were hilarious and she slept a lot through the pain, especially in her neck and head where the painful tumours grew very large, and were very visible to any visitor who sat to her right on her couch in the living room where she lay in her rented hospital bed.

I might add that her biggest fear wasn't of rapidly approaching Death, but rather how her boys would be cared for on Sept. 4th when the next school year would begin. I fought not to laugh out loud when Val concluded, "she wants you to know that she is 'back in control!' ". I guess there is a hot lunch programme, school dinner and dance committee and Special Olympics to plan and volunteer for on the other side too!

The kicker though, the real evidence was when Val left my flower she had so carefully placed on the podium and went on to another. She proceeded to apologize to whichever family she had moved on to and went back to Vicky's rose and said, "there is a red leather change purse with some kind of a medal inside, maybe a St. Christopher medal," making the gesture with her thumb and two fingers of closing a little change purse that we all had as little girls. I didn't know about that and was overwhelmed already with the accuracy of the reading. I was at peace knowing Vicky was safe, happy and back in charge in her new home. The school year began on September 4th, quite smoothly for Hayden and Hunter. They are loved by our staff beyond, beyond. One September day, Hayden thanked me most sincerely for the kindness shown to his family. He wheeled away and I took a breather to collect myself in an empty office. I texted Lori, Vicky's Best Friend and PSW who helped care for her friend and was helping Dave care for the boys, especially Hayden's special needs. I texted her cold, completely out of the blue, no mention of Vicky or the flower reading, asking if she knew of a red leather change purse.

Her response was, "Vic had a red leather change purse." I was so happy to be alone in that powerful moment. I did end up telling Dave all about Val and the flower reading, as well as my message and response from Lori. He cried the whole time. He remembers that red leather change purse too. He promised to give it to me whenever he finds it. For him, the thing that struck him was her message of being back in control. Her cancer eventually conquered her and left her powerless, even to speak. From total control, to none. He said that bothered her more than any amount of pain she endured. He said he felt total relief and eternal peace with this message from his wife. I am truly forever changed and blessed by both my time with Vicky in this life and through Val's extremely powerful, channeled message from my dear friend, Vicky.

...

APPORTS I HAVE RECEIVED.

Apports have been proven, through the centuries, to be gifts from Spirit, generally thought to appear during séances, but, wherever there is a medium who has the gift of physical mediumship an apport can appear spontaneously, anywhere and at any time.

When people are grieving, they often send their thoughts to their loved ones, in Spirit, and ask for a sign and many times their wishes are granted.

Sadly, because fake mediums, mentalists and magicians have used their tricks to produce so-called materialised articles, claims of their sudden appearance have been subject to ridicule.

This is understandable and I would encourage everyone to have a healthy skepticism about this, as I encourage everyone to test mediums at all times. In the case of apports please research every means of the article having been placed there by a physical person, to eliminate every doubt. To KNOW you have received an apport is so very precious, truly a gift from a loved one.

If a person has physical mediumship there will have been instances, during earlier life usually, when there has been unexplained energy around them. Since I was a child there has often been a freezing cold breeze around me that other people have felt, analysed and checked that it was not from, for example, an open window or draught from somewhere.

I have received 5 apports to date, so on a personal note I can attest to the fact that they do happen.

 The first was a cross which "appeared" in my then husband's tool box in the garage, it later literally vanished The second was a butterfly brooch that I'd had, which mysteriously vanished for 6 weeks, then re-appeared in my bed. You'd be forgiven for thinking that I'd just misplaced my jewellery, before coming across it again, after stripping back the sheets, but that wasn't the case in this instance. The third was a propelling pencil (an old fashioned type of pen but using very fine pencil) . It just appeared by my bed. The fourth was a packet of tissues (yes that is right, just ordinary everyday tissues for blowing your nose.) I was in the USA, in Tennessee. My friend Dianne and I were out shopping, as usual. I had a very bad cold and spent the whole day blowing my nose as it was running constantly. At one point having used all my tissues, I began using toilet paper. I gathered it from every shop and cafe we visited. We went for lunch, so I put my jacket on the back of the chair. After lunch, when I picked up my jacket, I reached into my pocket and took out two hands full of wet tissues and amongst them was a little plastic packet of clean tissues. I knew I didn't have any tissues in my pockets or my hand bag. I asked Dianne if she had put them there. "No, she said, I have never seen those before".

When I looked at the packet, although the writing on the front was in English, all the other writing was from Slovakia, and here I was in Tennessee, USA, totally inexplicable but true. There was no explanation for this, as no one had touched my jacket. We joked that her husband, Vern, was still looking after us from Spirit, but, actually, I do believe that to be true.

The 5th and latest was in December of 2018, when I was staying with my friend Jeanne in the South of England. Jeanne and I have known each other for more than 30 years. She generously hosted mediums who served a Birmingham Spiritualist church she was a member of.

Jeanne was a sitter in a circle for a man who had been an amazing healer and Trance medium for many years, giving her love and energy to the medium.

During her lifetime she, herself, has had some very interesting experiences of a physical nature, and I will be including her story in this book.

I was visiting Jeanne for just two days, as I was on my way to work in Portsmouth Temple for the weekend. I'd got up on the first morning of my visit, sitting at the breakfast table, chatting about mediums, mediumship and some of the remarkable things we've been privileged to witness individually.

Our conversation turned to fairies, yes fairies! Fairies are something that many people say are the imagination of a child, but I have actually seen them in a church, dancing on a piano, clairvoyantly of course, but at the time they were very real.

You may doubt my sanity at this point but I will continue with my story. I was at the church to watch another medium work when my attention was drawn to the side. At first I could see lights but when I turned to look closer I saw 5 or 6 fairies, each a different colour, dancing together. It is a memory that will stay with me to my dying day. Jeanne then told me of a friend of hers who had also insisted she had seen a fairy.

I excused myself to make my bed and have a shower. I went

up to my bedroom and on the floor, quite near to the bed I found a little gilt fairy with a green ribbon on it. I went back downstairs to show it to Jeanne and ask if she had lost it. Her response was quite funny "I can assure you I would not have something like that" said she. I asked if perhaps her cleaner could have dropped it, but Jeanne replied that her cleaner hadn't been up there.

It seemed too simple just to say it was coincidental, bearing in mind the conversation we had just had and her emphatic response that she had never seen it before and that no-one else had used her spare bedroom for a long time.
We were both humbled and joyful to think that Spirit had given us a gift, having listened to our conversation. Now I look forward to anything else they choose to bring for me.

...

JULY 2019 THE FEATHER
In July 2019 I was working on Senior Citizens Week at the Arthur Findlay College, a wonderful week with so many true Spiritualists, most of them healers and mediums.
On day I was in the lecture room and during a break I was talking to a lady, sitting near to the large table which is in the window.

The lady suddenly said "Look, I have just seen that feather appear" I looked and saw a beautiful feather, very light and fluffy and white, but thought no more of it. As always, when there seems to be some sort of phenomena we checked, to find that there were no open windows. Obviously, it could not have come from outside.

Sadly, I often take such events for granted, instead of taking time to take a photo., register the time etc., as a researcher would do.

Some hours later I asked someone where the feather was and they said the lady I had been talking to had taken it to her bedroom. I spoke to the lady and asked her to bring it down.

I was surprised to see it had changed so much, it was no longer white and fluffy, or curled up as it had been originally, so I took a photo of it and told the lady she could keep it.

A few weeks later I did a demonstration at Castleford church and three ladies who had been on the week at the college said they had all witnessed the feather "appearing". It is always nice to get confirmation, and I am so grateful to Spirit every time it happens.

...

People often ask why do these simple articles appear, and I believe that Spirit bring them to us so we will research, will take time to sit in circle for them, will be willing to be patient, allow Spirit to blend our energies, and use us to help them prove to people in this physical world that the Spirit world is real, that it is a world of intelligence, that Spirit people do communicate , all of this encouraging those of us who have the gift of mediumship to be willing to allow those, in Spirit, with greater knowledge than we, to develop our gifts quite naturally. If you feel you have such gifts please give time to Spirit and let them help your gifts to progress. The world needs this truth right now.

...

JEANNE'S STORY

As so many of my stories are about friends in Spirit, I thought I would like to write about someone who is still very much alive. Her age has always been a secret, but she is the same age as the Queen and her mind is every bit as agile! She has an incredible wit and I am very proud to call her my friend.

We first met, in the late 1980's. She used to host the mediums who served Kings Heath church in Birmingham. I believe I wrote something about her in my first book. However, my reason for writing about her now is because she is one of our Spiritualist movement's unsung heroes, someone who has given years of time and energy to someone else to aid the progress of that person's mediumship. She had the great pleasure of sitting for the mediumship of a gentleman who had been a very good trance medium and trance healer, every week going to give her energy for his mediumship.

The rewards, for her, were very tangible. Without people like Jeanne our excellent physical and trance mediums would not have been able to work, because whilst the medium has the necessary energy, naturally, people like Jeanne also have physical mediumship that they are not, necessarily, meant to use for themselves but are to give to someone else. Such was the mediumship over 100 years ago, totally unselfish. My own trance and some aspects of physical mediumship thrived because of the unselfishness of the Jeanne's of this world.

Here is her story in her own words:

My spiritual journey started in the late 1970s when my father, a prolific reader, thrust a book in my hand and said "You must read this, there are things we don't know and things we're not meant to know".

The book was Healing Hands by George Chapman. I found it most interesting, returned it to my father and thought no more about it until a year or two later my ex-husband was diagnosed with liver cancer.

The only way I could think of helping him was through spiritual healing. Although it didn't save his life, I am sure it helped him.

It left me wanting to know more. I read books and discovered the whereabouts of spiritual churches in Birmingham where I lived, including Kings Heath Church, where I was privileged to meet some very gifted mediums and speakers, some of whom I hosted when they came from up and down the country to serve the Church. I was also able to hold "mini-seminars" from time to time in my home.

Over the years I have had many messages and experiences of one kind and another and have had to try and sort the wheat from the chaff. I realise that my experiences are only hearsay to someone else, but I felt I should document them in the hope that some of them at least will be found of interest.

In my Birmingham Home: I returned from work one evening and went to the kitchen, where there were two double wall lights with glass shades. One of the light bulbs wasn't working. I went to remove it, only to find it wasn't there! I eventually found it several feet away on the floor behind a small antique saucepan which was there as an ornament. I replaced the bulb, not very easy to manoeuvre inside the glass shade. The following evening, I found the replacement bulb not working; this time it had jumped out of the bayonet fitting, but it had been unable to negotiate its exit from under the shade. I put this down to insufficient energy!

However, energy had been involved in removing a bamboo plant container from the adjacent wall. It was on the floor, although the strong nail it had been hanging on for years was still intact.

Another example of energy being used was in the kitchen: My mother-in-law had once given me a timer in the form of a small copper saucepan. As I didn't use it as a timer, I had it hanging on the wall. One morning, having put some eggs on the cooker to hard-boil, I returned later to find the timer going round.

I had got to know Jim Anderson (a trance medium and healer) and his daughter Margaret, who became valued friends. They used to come around on a Sunday evening for an informal circle.

On this particular Sunday morning I was in the kitchen (the kitchen again!) doing some cooking. I realised the date was June 23rd, my father's birthday, so I mentally wished him a happy birthday.

I took a new tub of butter from the fridge, removed the lid and used what I needed. When I came to replace the lid it was nowhere to be seen. I searched high and low with no success.

In the evening, at the end of our quiet time Jim said "Your father's here. He thanks you for the thoughts. Object-movement-I was responsible. I never did find the lid!!

A dear friend and a very gifted man, Paul Crowther, agreed to take one of my gatherings at home. He arrived at midday, we went straight into the kitchen, where I had prepared a light lunch. After lunch Paul said that while I was clearing up he would go into the sitting room to get the feel of it prior to the meeting.

When I joined him he was excited. He pointed to the framed photograph of my father, together with his World War army medals and said "That man has been following me around since last Tuesday (5 days), he's even been with me in the toilet! Paul recognised the cap badge on my father's cap on the photograph.

My father, obviously knowing that Paul would be seeing me, was desperate to warn me about someone I employed as Sales Manager in my company. I had already had an indication during a previous sitting that this was so, but he was such a plausible and likeable chap that I had chosen to ignore the warning. However, my father, who couldn't tolerate dishonesty, was determined to get through to me somehow.

In the evening, after the seminar, Paul and I were relaxing in the sitting room, when he said "Your father's still here. He's taking me to his photo and saying "there should be another medal and a pip". I remember my father, who rarely mentioned his wartime experiences, telling me he had been recommended for the Military Medal towards the end of the war, but had never received it.

The pip was a mystery to me until some years later my cousin gave me another photograph of my father in officer's uniform – hence the pip! I never knew he had been commissioned.

The Sales Manager's days were numbered, an expensive lesson for me. I learned later that he had served time for other misdemeanors.

One Sunday evening Jim and Margaret Anderson and a respected Birmingham medium, Vi Shelton, joined me for a circle in my sitting room, which was totally blacked out. On opening my eyes as the circle was drawing to a close, I saw a bright blue light on the floor by Jim's chair. I thought it must be moonlight until I realised moonlight couldn't penetrate the blackout curtains.

Margaret and I both crawled over and put our fingers into the light, which proceeded to drip from our fingers! I had always understood that ectoplasm was white (I had seen that at Stansted Hall)

Some months later I was hosting a gifted and knowledgeable medium by the name of Arthur Pratt. I told him about our experience in the circle and he immediately said "the hierarchy is experimenting with a new kind of ectoplasm"

...

I was hosting Eric Hills one weekend. Eric was not a medium, but an amazing, unassuming man, who knew a thing or two about energies. He was downstairs giving healing to a visitor, during which time my bedroom lights came on, the energies involved must have travelled upstairs to switch my bedroom lights on!!

Some time later, I received a call to tell me that Eric had died. Next day the light bulb in my standard lamp (which was not switched on) exploded into a myriad of pieces. Eric's sister phoned me later that day and I told her what had happened. Her matter-of-fact comment was "Oh, that'll be Eric".

Examples of energy being used also came to light when I was staying with my in-laws in Cumbria, and there were sounds and movements in my bedroom. After two nights with identical happenings I mention this, only to discover that my in-laws and my son, an arch skeptic, had had identical experiences.

Stansted Hall

During a week at Stansted Hall as I was waking up I heard a "physical" voice in my right ear, very brief and intelligible. The next day the same thing happened.

On the third morning the voice clearly said "Hello there". Those two words told me who it was. I worked out that the communicator had had two practice runs before he was successful the third time.

...

I have been given many messages over the years, some meaningless, others of great value. Amongst the most valued evidence has been the conveying of a person's character and personality apart from any words conveyed through a medium, who would have had no previous knowledge of the communicator.

The Power of Thought
A few years ago I was very concerned about a family matter and was sending out thoughts for help with the issue. I firmly believe that the following incidents were to let me

know that my thoughts had been recorded. (The third incident is really interesting!)

1.   Preparing my lunch one day I took a tub of olives from the fridge, removed the lid and took the tub with the rest of my lunch into the adjoining room. On returning to the kitchen - no lid.

Weeks later I removed the heavy fitted cushions from the chair I had used for lunch that day and found the missing lid. There was no way it could have found its way accidentally.

2. I admit to being somewhat obsessive about things being in the right pace, so t spotted immediately one morning that a small china ornament was missing from its usual place on the tallboy in my bedroom. I was going away for the weekend, so on my return I started looking for a replacement. I found the missing ornament in the bathroom.

3. This is really interesting, as I believe it demonstrates just how powerful the power of thought really is.
Not long after events 1 & 2 I drove to Marks & Spencer's large store nearby to buy clothes. I was in the habit of parking in a small bay which - as it was furthest from the store entrance - was more likely to have a space. I always lined up my parking spot with a specific feature of the store building, which made it easy to locate.

On returning with my shopping - no car. I was horrified. There were two Polish car cleaners nearby, one of whom spoke English. He said that car theft "never happened". He stood close to me as I described the car and he confirmed that it was missing. He advised me to go to the store's main entrance and report it to Security. The security guard took details of the car and made his way to the spot, me trailing some way behind with my heavy shopping bag. As he arrived at the spot he lifted his arm and I could see the car. He gave me a somewhat withering look and tried to excuse me by saying "Well, it's a big car park".

Next day I decided to return some of my purchases. I parked in the same little bay, being even more careful to align the car with a distinctive part of the store building. As 1 left the store I remember thinking "Wouldn't it be awful if the same thing happened?"
Need I say more?

No witness that day. No alternative but to go to Security, praying that it wouldn't be the same man on duty. It was! When he saw me he said "Lost your car again?" I replied that it would be there when he got there. Of course it was. Now I had to try and work out what had happened.
It's one thing for small objects to be moved - but a car? The car was always there, but was my energy field influenced so that I was unable to see it? My next question - how was it that the car cleaner witness couldn't see it? Was it because he was standing within my energy field and his mind was also being influenced? If not, how did it happen?

...

(If you experiencing any such experiences, please investigate as Jeanne is always willing to do, Val)

...

UNTRUE ACCUSATIONS
In 2005 I was invited to work for an organization in Sweden, having worked on Swedish week at the Arthur Findlay College.
I was excited to be there and initially thought they were a wonderful group of people. I quickly realised that, as everywhere else when there is a group of people you often get those who wish to be in the position of those who run the organization. Two of the women in particular wanted this, while seeming to be the best friend of the organizer. I worked there, I think, twice when the organizer was there, and then on the last visit she was away, working elsewhere. As always, there were workshops and during one of them one of her "friends" asked if I would do table tilting. I was a little unsure because, every time I do it is because Spirit

have told me to do it, and on this occasion they had not. I had never felt such weird energy in all the years I have worked for Spirit and have not since, she and I sat at the table and for a very long time there was no energy at all. Eventually, it just seem to be dragged, but was very heavy. It did go to one young woman and I did give her a message which she later verified, but I was not happy and wondered if the original woman was, for some reason, trying to block the energy.

I did my work and on the last evening went to another person's house and we booked my flights for the next visit. All seemed well.

However, a few weeks later I received a letter from the organizer to say I had been accused of cheating and would not be allowed to go again. I was absolutely devastated! The very thought of people cheating makes me feel physically sick. The last thing I would ever do is abuse Spirit in any way. I am too afraid I would lose my gifts if I even thought of cheating. To me it never makes sense.

Of course, I wrote to her, said the accusations were untrue and why had they encouraged me to book flights for next time if what they said was true. They could have simply let me leave and not waste money on a flight I would not be taking.

I was so hurt I vowed never again to do table tilting for any group.

A few months later I was to work on Manchester week at the College, having done table tilting for them the previous year. They were all excited for me to do it again. On that occasion the table had done what we called a lap of honour, bowing down to each person in turn as a thank you.

Everyone said they had never felt love like it from Spirit! I told Bill McGee the organizer that I would not do it ever again, and he pleaded with me. Suddenly, I remembered that on the course was a man who was a police detective, a very good witness I thought, who would certainly verify if it was correct and say if it was not.

We had our table tilting, and everyone was thrilled, including the policeman who had a message. I was incredibly relieved that it had gone so well.

After I had done a closing prayer a lady came to me and said "I heard about the table tilting in Sweden and have been told you cheated. I cannot wait to get back there and tell the organizers the truth about you and your work " People sometimes forget that good mediums are sensitive and the more we work with the physical and trance energies the more sensitive we become.

To this day I do table tilting with groups, but only when Spirit tells me that they want me to do it.

...

A Haunting in Louisiana
So-called hauntings are always interesting. They take many forms, some visual, and some audible. I say "so-called" because very often the people who experience them are unhappy or disturbed, but there really are occasions when there genuinely is Spirit activity.

One of these was something I experienced in the 1990's when I was in the United States, invited by the Louisiana Society for the Paranormal.

I had a day off and a dear friend invited me to a champagne buffet, which was delightful. Louisiana is famous for fabulous food and fabulous hospitality, so I was delighted to go.

Later in the day a young woman who had had a reading with me telephoned to ask me if I would like to go for a drive. How kind I thought, little knowing that she, Cyndy, and her husband Sam had an ulterior motive.

We drove out to an area where there are many plantation homes, beautiful homes in wonderful grounds, many of them restored to their former glory. This particular house is called The Myrtles, and has a reputation for being a "haunted house". As this was my first visit to Louisiana, I knew nothing of the area and had never heard of the Myrtles.

We arrived and Sam asked if I could "get anything", in other words would I tune in to the energies in the house. I thought this strange and, actually, a little rude, to ask a guest to work during her day off and told him so, but, nevertheless there was a sudden rush of energy and information. I went from room to room giving information and evidence of previous inhabitants of this beautiful old house.

Sam was amazed by the information I was giving, and was busily writing everything down. I remember talking about the house being lost as a gambling debt on one occasion, on another occasion a man was killed on the veranda and on another occasion a man was shot on the seventh step. Sam validated all the information but said I was wrong about the step the man was killed on because he had been told it was in another place. At this point he asked when I had read about the Myrtles and the history of the house. I told him I did not think I was wrong and hoped he could verify the information. I was very annoyed and told him I thought it very rude to invite me to work on my day off, expecting me to give information and then accusing me of researching first, ridiculous as I had no idea where our "drive" would take us. Only Sam and Cyndy knew that. However, we became friends, on many other occasions going out to the Myrtles.

On one such occasion National Geographic asked if they could record my interaction with the Spirit people who were evident in the house. They arrived, went all over the house connecting all their equipment but, unfortunately, the atmosphere was dreadful. The young man who was the current owner behaved in a very strange fashion indeed, drinking copious amounts of champagne, and then leaving the room suddenly, his behavior so bizarre that it would have been impossible to have an evening with Spirit.

I told the young man he needed to change his life-style and attitude to life, or he would lose everything.

Sad to say he did sell it in the end because he simply lost control of his life. On more than one occasion he crashed his car while driving under the influence of drink, ruining his life as had previous owners of the house.

Was this a case of possession or was it simply one young man's way of not taking responsibility for his own life? Many times, we are told that people are possessed, but it is very rarely the case. Many people, who are unstable either due to drink or drugs, seem to adapt behavior similar to the behavior of past owners of the houses where they live. Shortly after this I gave a spontaneous reading to a previous owner of the Myrtles. I told him he should buy back the house and within 12 months it would make more money than he had dreamt of.

He did not believe me as he, too, had had unhappy experiences in the house but he did, eventually, buy the house, restored it to the beautiful old mansion it had been and within months many people were hiring it for weddings, and other functions and, as I said, the money came pouring in.

Later the house was sold to a couple with a child and I lost contact with it, but what wonderful memories I have of the way Spirit can bring alive memories.

...

MARSDEN, MARSDEN AND MARSDEN.
There is a general misconception about Spirit activity, many
people believing this is brought about by evil Spirits.
Having lived with someone whose behavior manifested
often as something "evil" I realized that he was simply a
tormented soul, not pleasant to live with, and with the
ability to draw to himself negativity much of the time. Very
often this is a type of untamed psychic energy. People can
learn to control it unless the problem is a manifestation of
mental instability.

A young man telephoned me, speaking very aggressively,
telling me his house was haunted and he and his wife had
had "everybody" to the house to deal with it. He further
insulted me by asking what I charged to go to "deal with it".
I told him this was part of my work and that I had never
charged anyone for this aspect of my work. Talking to Spirit
to ask why they are causing a disturbance is something I
love to do.

His home was about an hour away, so I made an
appointment to go and then hoped he would not be there
when I arrived!
I have always taken a witness when I have been to house
disturbances and particularly felt the need to on this
occasion.

The stories he and his wife told me were very unusual,
more than any other stories I had been told, so I must say I
was intrigued to find out the truth, and relieved to find she
was on her own when I arrived.

On one occasion, the young wife told me, she was cutting
up vegetables for dinner in the kitchen, putting them in
pans when her child called her. She ran out to attend to the
child and when she came back she said all the vegetables
were prepared and all the pans placed on the cooker!
It may sound far-fetched but that was not the only story.
This young woman, in her twenties, said she was really
frightened because on another occasion she told her child

to tidy the bedroom because it was in a terrible mess.
She then went across the small landing to the bathroom
and minutes later when she came back all the clothes were
in a perfectly neat pile and the pictures that were on the
wall were also piled up.

This young mother told me that many things happened,
always dramatic things and they had many witnesses.
I arranged to take a healer from the local church as a
witness. When we arrived at the house the young man was
not there, but there were neighbours and friends in the
house. I said I needed everyone but her to leave in order to
deal with the situation properly, telling her it was not a side
show.

I explained there was probably a Spirit person trying to get
their message across that they needed to speak to someone
who would understand them.

I asked to go through the house on my own and left the
healer with the young mum. As I walked into the living
room, I saw a chaise-long under the window this was a
Spirit vision, they did not have a chaise-long)
A little girl was looking out of the window. She said "my
name is Jane Marsden" and then showed me how it looked
in Victorian times when she had looked out of the window.
She then told me a lot of things which I cannot remember
now. She talked about being the daughter of someone
locally and the young mother took notes of it all, later
checking in Parish records to found out that everything I
said was correct.

I talked about a specific picture they would be able to see,
or a photograph and this girl was on it.
The young couple of the house researched, found the
picture and later found the grave as well.
I asked Jane why she was causing so much disturbance and
she said that she was looking after the people, not only in
this house but in other houses on the street.

She then told me that there was a young woman across the road who was pregnant and she was afraid she would lose the baby. She said that the young woman had lost one baby, was afraid she would lose this one and she asked that someone would go to tell her she would not lose this baby. The young woman whose house I was researching did go over the road and as I asked said "you've had some sort of disturbance in your house like me haven't you? I have had a medium to the house and she says you are not to worry about the baby you are carrying. It will be alright." Apparently, the poor girl went as white as a sheet. She said nobody knew she was pregnant to which the other young woman said "Well the little girl Jane did"

I was also given from Spirit "Marsden, Marsden and Marsden" and so I asked the young woman of the house what it meant to her. She literally drained of colour, then told me that her partner and she were moving to a house in Marsden, her partner had been out of work and had just got a job at Marsden's and that mill owners owned a good portion of the land, which is why they could verify my information within the Parish records.

Just before I left, I said that when I first arrived in the house I had seen a big man in the kitchen, who looked like a farmer. I described him and again the young woman drained of colour. She said she had actually seen him so I was able to reassure her that he would not do any harm, he just wanted to be there and would make sure everything was alright for them.

To this she replied "Oh, I don't mind then"
I did not think there would be further problems but said they could contact me if there were any. To this date I have heard nothing from them. I will always be grateful to Jane Marsden for confiding in me.

...

2018-THE CHRISTMAS GIFT

This was a year of ups and downs, but a year in which I probably learnt more about myself than at any other time. The year started very well. My friend Marianne came to England and we had a wonderful week together, no work, just two women having fun, going to shows, but as often happens we could not ignore the needs of other people, so we visited some sick friends together as well.

We are both healers and could not be true to Spirit had we totally ignored the needs of those who needed healing, even if that simply meant visiting them.

In March I looked forward to my annual seminar at the Lindum Hotel in St.Anne's, which has been running for just over 30 years, but this one was to be more special as I was to celebrate a big birthday while we were there. I was planning not to work, just to organize the weekend, and enjoy the company of people. Why do we ever think we can plan anything?

As so often happens there were many changes. It snowed in almost every part of England, so 30 of my people could not possibly travel and two of my mediums were snowed in as well, so I had to totally reorganize and I had to be one of the tutors taking a group.

I should have realized then that I would have to be very flexible for the rest of the year.

In March I did a demonstration for Barrow in Furness Spiritualist church which was trying to build itself up again. The small committee were working so hard and continued to do so but, sadly, it has since had to close.

June began a domino effect which, now in 2020 seems not to have ended. My lovely friend Lynette passed to Spirit, having been in hospital for 9 months. The day before her funeral I received word that another dear friend had had a massive stroke, and the day after that a seemingly fit and healthy 50 years old friend had a heart attack. I found myself visiting more people in hospitals, writing more get-well cards than usual and generally stretching myself as much as humanly possible.

August was a total nightmare- I decided to have 5 weeks off work in order to write this second book, but Spirit had other ideas. Every day I found myself needing to help someone, visit sick people, listen to people's problems etc.
In September I went to Longton church, a church I have not served for many years, and stayed with the lovely couple who run it together with a hard-working, stable committee. It was thrilling to talk to them and know that they, like me, want to uphold all the old Spiritualist truths, training, and dignity, as well as adapting to the Modern age.
In November, having had to cancel one of the mediums for very good reason which I explained to him in detail, I booked two female mediums who I had worked with many times, and Sally Barnes from Norwich was also to work. Suddenly there was a rush of people booking to come to the seminar, the whole energy had been changed and we shared a wonderful weekend together.

I always feel it important, during seminars, to work hard and have fun after work. During the November seminars we have a very silly, funny exchange of Christmas gifts during which the most serious person ends up laughing and the most Spiritual show their inner child, all in all a weekend not to be missed.

After all the stress, sadness and irritations of the year I was looking forward to the end of the year and a new one beginning but then Spirit had a plan I was unaware of.
A SPECIAL CHRISTMAS GIFT I was planning to go to a wonderful restaurant with friends, for a pre-Christmas meal in Whalley, a village in Lancashire. We arrived, ordered our meal and were just chatting. It was a great atmosphere and the place was tastefully decorated. We were sitting in a bay window and there were lights and candles in the shape of stags on the windowsill.

We were talking about a person who had created some dreadful problems for other people and as his name was mentioned one of the stags seemed to throw itself off the windowsill.

The funny part of this is that the wife of one of our friends is not involved in the work her husband does for Spirit and yet here she was with the perfect view of the thing throwing itself. The rest of us, all believers and all of us having had our own experiences just saw it after it fell. Her face was a picture I must say, and I have a feeling Spirit needed her to be the one to see it happen to validate her husband' Mediumistic ability and I believe it was also the means of the Spirit operatives to encourage her to open herself up to whatever Spiritual abilities she may have herself.

I did check that the lady sitting with her back to the window could not have knocked the candle off. Her chair had certainly not touched either the window sill, or the little string of lights, and the candle was so heavy the string of lights could not have caused it to fall or throw itself across to our table anyway.

Just before we had sat down a friend had sent a text to tell me her dad had just died. He was very ill and was expected to pass. We arranged to meet up and during the course of our visit I told her about the "flying stag" at Breda Murphy's. That is funny, she said, I was there with my sister last week for my birthday lunch. I asked was she sitting in the bay window, to which she replied "no, at the little table to the side" – coincidence. Maybe, I don't have all the answers, but I had just heard that her dad had passed to Spirit and she later told me that he used to go out hunting deer and that he had them mounted on the wall in his home.

I think that for all of us it was a particularly wonderful Christmas Gift, something that could not be bought in a shop but which Spirit gave to us.

I will never have all the answers to some of the things that happen but it is certainly fascinating and never a boring journey.

STANSTED TABLE TILTING.

I have so many stories of table tilting, a means of communication that is often misunderstood by people who use it as a toy, a play thing. I have lost count of the number of people who say "oh how exciting it is". When done properly the energy is exciting, but behind the excitement there is an intelligence manifesting from the Spirit world and my love and respect for this intelligence is my only reason for doing table tilting.

Many people, using their own psychic energy, create a psychic energy which causes the table to appear to run round, sometimes in circles, but without great purpose. For the purpose of workshops or demonstrations during seminars my Spirit workers devised a system of table tilting during which two people sit at the table, a prayer is said as a mark of respect for Spirit, and then when ready the table may seem to dance and move around the room. Two people keep their hands right on top, never putting their thumbs under the edge of the table. At some point the table will go to someone sitting in the circle and they then place their hands on it. The two people originally on will then tune in to Spirit and channel a message for this person, giving evidence of Spirit.

It has been this means of communication which has made many people change their minds about what they sometimes thought were people cheating or that it was just a game. Of course, there has been cheating during the years but when it is genuine there is a special type of energy, a positive, loving energy.

One such person, now a good friend, came on a course with his girlfriend, not believing in much of what we do as mediums. He is often heard to say that when he did table tilting with me he knew what was real. (See Tim Smith's testimonial)

Another person, a lady who is now a good medium herself, wrote to me after her session to say she had never done table-tilting before. Her husband had died many years previously and for the first time she felt his love, through a piece of wood. Apparently I told her that her sons would speak to each other after 17 months (not knowing she had sons or anything about her). 18 months later she wrote to say that her sons, who had not been speaking to each other, had spoken, which backed up her belief that her husband was helping her behind the scenes. Since this time she has lost her eldest son and so I feel it was vital she had this experience, to know her boy is now safe in the Spirit world, no doubt with his father.

There have been so many occasions that this means of communication has helped people and I usually have one evening of Table tilting during my seminars for those who wish to take part.

However, April 2018 was truly the icing on the cake. I had a group of about 24 people, so there was just myself and one other medium for the week. I decided to have a table tilting session in the lecture room, so after the day's work in the lecture room I prepared the room as always, setting the chairs in a big circle, with the small table and two chairs in the middle. I also left music on to create a nice atmosphere. The evening went ahead as usual and at one point there were two small round tables with students on, they giving messages to the recipients who had been invited to put their hands on by Spirit.

I was then impressed to go to sit at the huge old-fashioned dining table which is in the window of the lecture room. As I placed my hands on it I could feel an undulating energy, so I called my colleague to sit the other side of the table and we could both feel an energy flowing between us.
I was then impressed to invite students to come on the table, one by one until we were 13 people. The energy was wonderful! Suddenly I knew Spirit were ready, so I told everyone to stand up, and very soon the huge, heavy table moved very slowly until it was in the very centre of the room. It stopped under a large light, which made me think

that as this had been Arthur Findlay's dining room, maybe this is where the table used to be in his day.

Some of the students started to sing the Bee Gees song "Staying alive" and with no warning the table started rotating very quickly and thirteen of us were running round with it, the energy was fabulous!

Suddenly it just stopped, all energy going from it. All I could think was that I would be in trouble if we could not get the table to go back to where it had come from!
I said to Spirit "If this has been moved by the intelligence of Spirit you must now put it back exactly where it came from". Nothing happened! I asked everyone to take their hands off the table. For some heart-stopping minutes again, nothing happened. When I felt the energy building up I asked my colleague to put her hands back on the table. Immediately we could feel the presence of Spirit, so, one by one I asked the other 11 people to put their hands on. After a short time, the table moved little by little back to the alcove from where it had come and finally came to a halt very, very close to its original position.

Everyone was euphoric, no one spoke! It was one of those glorious moments that needed no words, truly a gift from Spirit for all of us.

As I explained to the students, they really were one of the nicest groups of people I had ever had at the college and I believed this was a gift to them, giving them a true understanding that when we work together and respect each other Spirit will reward us.

There was, of course a follow-up to this story, because my colleague suddenly pointed up to a security camera on the ceiling.

The next morning my colleague and I saw the assistant manager and told her what had happened. She immediately said she wanted to see it for herself, as she couldn't believe it. Later the manager came, a gardener, the maintenance man, and others. Everyone watched the coverage on two monitors. They were all in shock as many of the people who work there are not Spiritualists and have little understanding of what we do.

I believe that later a few of them went into the Lecture room, put their hands on the table and tried to move it. Of course, it would not move, it is too heavy, but I am glad they tried.

Most amazing to me was that this heavy table left no mark whatsoever on the carpet, despite it having Victorian castors on the legs of the table.

I had so hoped to have a recording of the whole séance (which was held in broad daylight on a sunny afternoon and with the curtains open) Unfortunately my colleague and I have only been given a couple of minutes of it, but we are thrilled to have that.

Nothing can take away the honour of being allowed to take part in the most amazing séance.
If you wish to try this yourself, please always do so for the right reasons, respect Spirit and ask for evidence each time you do it.

What I know for a fact, having had physical mediumship all my life, is that when the right group of people come together, they are brought together by Spirit.
There is a follow-up to this story, something equally as evidential and exciting but that must wait for Book 3!

...

THE TRAVELLING MEDIUM
The life of an "International Medium" is all that is sounds and much more. I remember friends warning me about the perils of travelling, of staying in other people's homes and I thank God that most of the time I was alright.

There have been horrific stories such as one medium who was invited to Kuala Lumpur. Her hostess only gave her food on the days she worked, she slept in a bed that had more sand fleas than feathers in the mattress, and she watched praying mantis' climb her curtains. The poor medium ended up with double pneumonia and almost died. Other mediums have worked in foreign countries and having been invited to dinner were suddenly pounced upon by the host who demanded that they gave each guest a message from the Spirit world.

GERMANY
I remember my first working visit to Germany. A friend who regularly went there could not go at the last minute and asked if I could go in her place. Having a free week, I agreed, feeling very excited at the prospect of meeting new people. I was collected at the airport and delivered to the place I would sleep, a beautifully clean guest house. The owner proudly showed me the Television which had an English channel. It just happened to be something called MTV and was the worst music I could imagine, but it was a very nice place and the whole area looked lovely, clean and very pretty.

When I was taken to my hosts' house to do readings, she told me she would interpret every sitting as the people did not speak English. I learnt very quickly that occasionally translators do not faithfully repeat what they hear and this was one such experience.

On one such occasion I felt sure she had said far more than I had said to the client. I asked her what she had said to which she indignantly asked why I needed to know. I explained that to change the word of Spirit could be to mislead the client. She told me that she was simply telling the sitter what God wanted her to do! I said this was not acceptable. She was quite furious with me.

On another occasion a young man came to me for a sitting, his wife and children waiting in another room. The young man had obviously had a stroke, had difficulty walking and had the typical dead-weight arm of a stroke victim. During the sitting my Voice said he would like to give the man healing should he like to have it. I mentioned this to the translator and she told me he would like to have healing. I duly gave him healing time after the sitting and then was aware of what she was asking him even though I did not speak her language. When I asked her what she wanted from him she said, "I am telling him how much it is for the healing". I was very upset because I would never offer healing to some-one, and then expect money for it. I told her there was no charge and she said "whenever I give healing, I charge the patient". I quietly pointed out to her that she had not done the healing, that Spirit had offered it and used me to give it and there was NO charge. She was even more furious with me.

On another occasion she pointed to someone in the street and said "tune into that person and tell me what you think of them because I do not like them" Naturally I refused, explaining that I did not use my mediumship in that way, ever, not even if I wanted to know about someone for myself.

Am I surprised she did not ask me to work for her another time? No!
Am I happy she did not ask me to work for her another time? Oh Yes!!
Very, very rarely people try to use mediums for their own ends, maybe to promote themselves as mediums, to try to increase their social status or simply because they want messages for themselves.

All would be hosts should realize that good mediums are

good mediums because they value and appreciate the gifts they have. Many of us have at some time been ill-used. We may allow ourselves to be used once, but the lesson is then learnt.

FUNNY MOMENTS
In 2005, having worked for Spirit for many years, I was reasonably well known and reasonably respected. I have enjoyed almost every day of my work for Spirit, much of it is challenging but I have always been determined to be the best medium I could for Spirit, not in competition with anyone else, but for myself and for Spirit.

The general public, particularly those who do not understand mediumship, seem to think that being a medium means you are someone special, someone to be revered. That is a silly trap that many mediums fall into when in early development of their mediumistic gifts.
A medium is simply someone who is developing their gift of mediumship, a GOOD medium is someone who works for the world of Spirit and who gives honestly what they receive to recipients of the messages. Development never finishes.

After each opportunity to work, whether publicly or privately, the Medium simply reverts to being a person who has a life in the physical world, the appointment times bringing the two worlds together.

There have been so many times during the past 40 years that have showed me the ego has no place in the life and world of a medium who truly works for Spirit.
I remember the time I was in Grimsby church, waiting to start my demonstration. I overheard a conversation between two young women that went something like this:
"Do you know who is on tonight?"
No – do you?
"No, I was going to go to the pub tonight instead of coming here so I hope she is good"
Oh, well, we can go to the pub after.......................................

74

Five minutes later I was to start my demonstration but before I did I recalled the conversation for everyone to hear, and then turned to the girls and said "mine's a brandy and dry ginger". This brought much laughter and took away any embarrassment the girls may have felt.

...

On another occasion I was asked to go to a hotel in Blackpool, to do a reading for the mother of a famous Northern comedian. I arrived with Muriel, who often accompanied me. We had a little chat with a mutual friend who had brought the lady to the hotel and then, in private, I gave her a reading for about half an hour.

After it was finished, knowing I had given good evidence, I took the lady back to our friends. The lady looked at Muriel and said "when are you going to give me my reading then?" We were all absolutely amazed. She obviously didn't realize that I had just done her the reading. What she thought I was telling her I have no idea!

When we asked her why she thought Muriel was the medium and I was not, she said it was because I was blonde and Muriel had dark hair.
Thankfully, we all had a good laugh about it and then went to lunch.

...

There have been many occasions when I have been over-looked as a medium. Many people's perspective is still to believe that a medium is someone who tells fortunes, wears hoop ear-rings and has coins along her forehead, like the typical picture of the old Romany gypsies.

...

How well I remember, during the first two years of developing my mediumship, the time I was describing a Spirit lady to someone in Fleetwood church. I was giving very detailed evidence and finally I said "she is showing me how she made the bed, with beautifully white, perfectly ironed sheets. She always threw the sheets up in the air before she made the bed"

"Oh, I know who that is, said the recipient, but she is dead!" Everyone in the church laughed and I tried to keep a straight face as I said "I only pass on messages from dead people".

...

HAPPY DAYS
There are so many misconceptions about the life of a medium-often people believe that when we travel at home or abroad, we are hosted at the finest hotels.

We are usually invited to the home of someone from the church, which most of the time is lovely. I have stayed with many people, during the years, with whom I have formed a strong bond, have become part of their family, and been able to relax in their company.
However, on one occasion my hostess badgered me every moment because she wanted me to give her a reading. I finally gave in, did her reading at 8am, and left without breakfast, never to return. It was a very long time before I told the church officials why I had not wanted to return to their church.

Another time, having become great friends with a couple from the Midlands, the wife told me that her husband had flirted with me the following evening. Not finding him the least bit attractive I had not even noticed!

I have stayed in poor homes, and homes of very wealthy people, none of that mattering, just feeling at home is lovely and the atmosphere in that home determines whether I enjoy my mediumship or not.

When I first went to Burslem a lady called Freda hosted me. It was my first visit and I had been told she was vegetarian so I took my own food with me. I did the church service, went home to her house and at 7am the following day she knocked on the door to say her daughter had had a baby prematurely during the night and could I look after myself so she could go to the hospital. I laughed and told her I was a big girl.

Later in the day we went back to the hospital where I met the baby and Freda's daughter. To this very day Freda and I are close friends, more like a mother and daughter relationship, our initial bonding partly due to the baby's arrival, our other connection being Barry Manilow music, which at the time we both loved.

...

An experience that was not such a happy one was when I stayed with a lady I had stayed with many times. Her house was very dirty but I liked her very much. I always made sure we ate out. However, the final straw, and the experience which made me not want to stay again was when I was covered in flea bites. She had cats, had realized there was a problem, but had done nothing about it.

Oh, well, I can imagine some of you thinking. You are so well paid that should not matter. Not quite true I assure you. In the 1980's to be paid £5 for a service seemed like a lot of money, as some churches only paid £2. How many of you would spend a day travelling to a venue, give two days of your life for £10 plus your petrol money, and then drive home, taking another day out of your life? £10 for 4 days did not pay the bills even in those days.

The tax officer was very confused as to why anyone would "work" for such little money but I can honestly say I have never worked just for the money. In fact there have been times when I have done readings for people and at the end my voice has said "you cannot charge this person any money". This has usually been when someone has lost a child or is very newly bereaved and not able to cope with life at all. I usually say they should just take their money and buy flowers from their loved ones, as a gift from them.

...

The reverse of this has been, on occasion, when people say they cannot afford to pay for a reading. On each occasion when this has been said I have found it not to be true. In fact I have found that desperately grieving people would never say they cannot afford it, even if they cannot. They will save and save their money until they can afford it. One such lady was a client in Canada very recently. She had contacted me to ask if there was a reading available because she had lost her daughter and was not coping at all. Despite being fully booked, I felt it was right to do it as my last one of the day.

The poor lady cried from start to finish, unselfishly accepting that her daughter had to die because it was her time, and yet grieving so desperately. She was thrilled with the evidence her daughter gave to me to pass on, and at the end my "voice" told me to make sure she got her money back.

Asked the lady who was hosting the readings to return the sitters money, she gave the lady her money back and the lady said "oh, the medium must have known how hard up I am".

No, of course, I did not know, but I never defy my voice. This has not been the first time it has happened and it will not be the last.

...

On a seminar in the early 90's a man who was attending a seminar said he thought it was disgraceful that mediums charged money for their gifts.

I told him I absolutely agreed with him and that I had recently telephoned the gas company to say I could not pay for the gas they supplied me with because I was a medium and so should not charge for my gift, which meant I had no money to pay. He got the message!

Mediums and healers are entitled to charge for their time. Nobody can buy healing or mediumship. As Gordon Higginson said to me in 1982 "The labourer is worthy of his hire". I believe it is the right of the worker for Spirit to make their own choice.

I have already mentioned that one of my favourite places to work in the 1990's and onwards was Denmark, each year doing demonstrations and readings.

I gave a message to a lady during a public demonstration, giving incredible evidence about her son, the link starting because I said I had a young man with me, someone's son and his mother had kept his sweater. The lady, right at the back of the hall, held up her son's sweater and then was able to have very personal evidence.

Some days later a man came for a reading. He was not Danish but Scottish, and he was, apparently the father of the boy. He had a 45 minute reading, said "yes" many times, and then right at the end told me he did not think I was linking with his son, despite many personal pieces of information including their joint involvement with music. I told him not to pay for the reading and he asked where was the person who had arranged the readings. I pointed him in the direction of the organizer, carried on with my work, and later, when all the readings were finished, she pushed some money towards me I said, surely you have not taken money from that man when he said he did not believe I was talking with his son, to which she replied that yes, she had, telling him that he was to pay for my time. What really saddened me about this experience was the sadness I felt from his son in Spirit, and the disappointment he felt in his father.

This behaviour is very rare, fortunately, meaning there are so many wonderful occasions when I feel the pure joy, when a living person accepts the information, evidence and love from the Spirit communicator.

MY CANADIAN FAMILY

My love affair with Canada began back in the late 1990's when I worked in the Vancouver area. It is quite normal to be invited to stay in the home of someone from the hosting church, and I was hosted beautifully.

In 2007 I should have been working at the Arthur Findlay College on a week that had to be cancelled. I received a call asking if I would be willing to run a week, but they would have no time to advertise it as the course was two weeks later. I was happy to agree, the course was put on the SNU Website and two weeks later I presented myself to be the course organizer and tutor, little realising, at the time, that I would be the only tutor for the whole week.

There were 16 students, from all over the world and they gave themselves the title "The Stansted 16", many of them still keeping in touch with each other.
One of the people was a lady who was from Ontario, a pleasant person who blended in very well with the other people. Apparently, she had come to England, having been in Europe with her daughter because she saw it as a good opportunity to visit the world- famous Arthur Findlay College, renowned for its teaching and good standard of mediumship.

At the end of the week she said that if I was ever in the Toronto area, I should call her and perhaps the local church would ask me to do something for them. At no time did she tell me her role in the church. I will call her Betty for the purpose of the book.

A few months later I was asked to attend a conference in Rochester, New York State and, having no idea of distance, I contacted Betty, told her where I was to go and she immediately invited me to stay with her and her family, and later I was invited to do a little work for the church.
That was the start of a long association with the church, many happy hours spent there, tutoring students, doing demonstrations, helping and advising when asked. In fact, I

felt very much at home there, sharing as much of my knowledge with Betty as I could. I was happy to help and advise her as much as possible because she seemed to be very passionate about the Pioneers of Spiritualism and the phenomena that were created during the early years. I always went the extra mile for her and the church, did Trance demonstrations, table tilting workshops and physical mediumship experiments, sharing as much of the knowledge Spirit had given to me as was possible.

Each time I visited the church the number of people attending increased dramatically and when the time came for the church to move to a bigger building my visits were so popular that it was usual to have over 50 people for a Sunday service and once when I did a flower service there were over 80 people, many more than there had been before I started working for them. The church flourished for a time, but sadly over a period of about 5 years many people left the church, many who had worked for the committee moved on, and the atmosphere changed. During the last two visits it became obvious that I would no longer be able to work there so, with a great feeling of sadness, I cancelled my next booking at the church, and then left it to Spirit to lead me to wherever they wanted me to be.

As well as having had a good working relationship with the people at the church I had a wonderful connection to Betty's family in Spirit. During most visits we would go to her holiday home and, while there, we would use the glass and the letters, encouraging Spirit to communicate with us in this way. Betty had many evidential messages during those times and, invariably she would ask me to do a reading for her, which was always special because it was a place her parents had loved.

Feeling family love
I would often do sittings for Betty and her family when I was in Ontario. I felt they were like family to me so I always charged the young people "family rate" and of course I

never charged Betty at all as she was a generous host.

I knew her lovely mum but, sadly, never met her dad who she adored. Luckily for me he loved communicating to his daughter and seems happy to give me messages for her, sometimes amazingly accurate evidence.

One of the messages that, to me, was incredible was when she was having a lot of stress at work due to a new boss. It doesn't really matter what the stress was, needless to say it was making her feel very uncomfortable every day, not an easy environment to work in.

During our regular sitting her dad said to me that her boss would leave the job at Easter. When messages are as precise as this I often worry, in case I get it wrong. After all these years I should know better, but very often these are life-changing messages.

Once I was back home, I kept checking with Betty, by e mail, to find out if her boss had left yet and each time it was "no". Finally, I got an e mail telling me that he left on Good Friday, so the message was true and I was very relieved.

If information given to a recipient is NOT pure evidence from Spirit, and if what is promised does not happen it can totally destroy the belief system of the recipient. Very often the recipient will then say that "Spirit got it wrong" instead of blaming the medium, who may not be developed enough, or may simply say things that the recipient wishes to hear. The person who claims to be a medium simply passes on what has been said by a communicator. A psychic on the other hand reads the energy field of the recipient and can often give untrue or misleading information.

I thank God every day that I have natural mediumship, my training totally done by Spirit, from when I was a small child, even if I did not understand any of it until I was 33.

I am constantly surprised by Spirit when I realise how much help and support they have been in my life, and looking back I am eternally grateful to them.

I had a very unhappy childhood, living with parents who hated each other. I don't remember them speaking to each other, though they were together 24 years and 9 months. My mother told lies about me to my father, saying I never helped when in fact I did the shopping from the age of 8, babysat my younger sister so my mum could go out dancing when my dad worked away, and cleaned the house when she would not.

My dad worked away for weeks at a time. He was a deep-sea fisherman when I was young, later on having jobs which allowed him to be home more often.

Once, when my mother had a broken leg, and I was 13 years old he came home and she started screaming that I had done nothing to help, despite my having done everything as usual. This strong man with his big hard hands hit me so badly I wet myself. I have never forgotten the embarrassment of standing there in the kitchen. I don't know which was worse, being accused of something I had not done, or wetting myself. From that day until I was 22, I spoke not one word to him. It took many years to accept that the person who was really in the wrong was my mother.

So, after an unhappy childhood, followed by an abusive relationship with a psychotic, sometimes, violent husband, I emerged at the age of 42 having known not one day of love in my life.

Thank God for Spirit and their allowing me to work for, and with them, because I managed with their help to turn everything around.

Although I have very little contact with my birth-family I have friends all over the world who are my Spiritual family and that sustains me through the lonely and difficult times. I mentioned earlier Betty and her lovely mum, such a sweetheart. On one visit I was picked up from Toronto airport as usual. Betty said her mum was dying but she was sure she had waited for my visit. We went directly to her house and I was able to sit with her for a couple of hours.

She died the next day and I was asked to do a service for her at the church, such a privilege. She has since communicated her messages to the family she loved so much which was always an honour and pleasure for me because I got to speak with her again. She was a wonderful mum in life and I was allowed to feel a beautiful love from her when I communicated messages to her family, something I never experienced in my own family.

...

This brings me to some questions for you:
If you have not come from a loving family are you able to give and show love to others?

If you were not loved as a child have you yet found confidence in yourself so you know you are lovable?
Has anyone from the Spirit World made you feel more loved than you have ever felt from the physical world?
As a medium have you given a communication when the purest of love has shown you what is real?
I hope that you have been able to answer "yes" to these questions as I can. Remember our existence in this physical world is for a brief time – eternity is for ever. It naturally follows that whatever we can learn and feel in this lifetime will encourage our progress in the Spirit world when we "go home".

Many of the negative emotions, thoughts and feelings we may have during this lifetime really are experiences to learn from, to be able to survive and as we move forward, we are able to help others, give love to others and in turn receive some love we so badly need.

Unfortunately, my connection with that particular family is now severed but I will remember, forever, the love I felt, of a husband to his wife, and of a mother to her daughter, such a blessing and I thank God every day that I survived the conditions of my earlier life.

Freedom is sometimes something we must fight for but it is

truly worth the fight.

...

When I first visited the church, which was a large detached house, I used to stay in an apartment that was above the church hall, but once the church was sold I was to stay with a lady who was on the committee, little knowing how close Pat and I would become. Pat is one of those very high energy people who can turn her hand to anything: painting walls, knocking nails into walls, sewing, crafts etc., and much of this benefitted the church for many years.

My very first visit to Pat's home was quite a revelation because on her coffee table I was astonished to see a little book depicting Tenbury Wells, which is a village, in England, about 10 minutes from my friend Joyce, who is mentioned in the chapter on Earth Angels.

Pat told me her husband Bob was from Tenbury Wells, that he had moved to Canada to work and that the minute she met him she knew he would be the man she would marry. Sadly, Bob had died before I stayed with Pat, but apparently, I had given him a message during one of the services at her church. Though he had never lived in the house Pat moved to after the death of her beloved Bob his presence is often felt in the home she shares with her daughter, son in law and two lovely children. I am happy to say they have become my Canadian family.

Pat has her own story of having had a reading with me, shortly after Bob died and I quote:
The first time I had a reading with Val, was at the old Spiritualist church. My daughter Erin and I booked appointments with Val. Erin was booked in at 11am and I was booked at 11.30. When we got to the church Erin asked me to go in first. When I walked in Val said to me – you are Pat (she should have said you are Erin who was booked for 11am) I said yes, I am. Val said "I have something here from your husband" I said that was nice but told her my husband had passed to Spirit.

Val said "I know that, but he wouldn't let me leave England without this". She then handed me a package of Penguin Biscuits. My husband was born and raised in England and loved Penguin bars.

To many people this would not have been very evidential but to Pat is certainly was.

I still go to Ontario each year, to stay with Pat and her family and I always take Penguin biscuits. The children love to read the joke that is on each biscuit and Pat loves the memory of her husband and his love of British biscuits.
Pat and I had talked, many times, of her coming to England to stay with me and as part of the visit we would have stayed with Joyce, all of us going to Tenbury Wells, which sadly did not happen, because Joyce died before Pat did come.
On her list of things to do before Pat died was a visit to Brugges, in Belgium. She fell in love with it when she saw a film which was set in Brugges. I had been there many years earlier and had absolutely loved it so we made that the main part of our planned trip, enjoying every single second. One of the highlights, for Pat, was that I insisted we went to the Menin Gate to see the memorial for all the people who had lost their lives during the war. The feeling there is quite wonderful and I would recommend everyone to visit. My favourite photo of Pat was taken when she pointed to the name of a relative who had died during wartime, a young man who had come from Canada in service to his country. Originally, Pat was going to come for a month but I was to have a big birthday celebration a few months later, so she cut her visit to three weeks so she could come again in March 2018, so I had to rethink and we prioritised the places she wanted to see.

We had often talked of Scotland, how beautiful it was and she had had relatives from there so it was important to include it in our itinerary.

It was during this trip that Bob chose to make himself known to us in the most wonderful way. This is Pat's report of the trip:

"In August 2017 I spent just over 3 weeks with Val. On the way to Dunfermline, where we were going to stay for a couple of days, we stopped to have lunch in Gretna Green, Scotland. As I was washing my hands I noticed that my Claddagh ring was missing. My late husband and I went to England and Ireland for our 25th wedding anniversary and he bought me the ring in Killarney, Ireland. Needless to say I was heart-broken about losing the ring but there was nothing I could do about it.(the ring has two hands holding a heart and a crown)We had stopped for petrol and a bathroom break just before crossing into Scotland so I figured that was when I lost it.

I told Val I was not going to let it spoil my trip to Scotland and if it was meant to come back to me it would do, that it was out of my control.

We had a wonderful time, visited Edinburgh and on the way back to England we were to stop at the same service station where I figured I lost my ring.

Just before we got to the service station Val said to me "Bob said you will find your ring". When we arrived, I asked the lady at the courtesy desk if anybody had turned in a Claddagh ring, described it to her. She called the Lost and found department but my ring was not there.
As Val and I were walking back to her car I said "Well Val, Bob was wrong about the ring – I didn't find it"
As I opened the passenger door, I saw something glinting at the back of my seat – it was my ring!! The sun was shining on it where it was wedged in the car seat.

We were in and out of the car many times while in Scotland. If the ring was there all the time I, would have seen it sooner. Val asked me if I had put my hands into the back of the seat, but I said I hadn't and if I had the ring would have been wedged in the seat band side up and not the Claddagh side up.

So, Val was absolutely right when she told me Bob said I would get my ring back, this in itself being a gift because these messages truly are gifts from Spirit, and I am very happy to have my ring back.

My friendship with Pat and her family is stronger than ever – I love staying with her, and keep in touch with many of the people I met when I first visited the Spiritualist church.

...

For the many years I visited the Ontario church I made many friends, and when I longer worked there I felt it necessary to suggest to four of my dear friends that, due to their involvement with the church we should distance ourselves from each other, but if they chose to reconnect at a later time I would be happy to resume our friendship. One couple chose not to continue with the friendship, which made me very sad because I had truly felt close to them and, in particular, to their lovely young son, who I believe I had been able to help. I will always remember my connection with them with a great deal of fondness, and wish them well in everything they do.

From the first time I met Walter and Krystyna, a lovely Polish couple who had lived in Canada for many years, we just connected.

Always able to laugh with each other, we enjoyed meals out and they came to my workshops, demonstrations etc., when I was in Ontario. When I first met them, they helped a church in London, Ontario, a lovely church to work at, and which I have recently done a service for, on Zoom.
Walter seemed quite shy, and a little out of his depth, obviously lacking confidence. Krystyna always had a great dignity, both of them being incredibly respectful to Spirit, loving every aspect of their development.

It was wonderful to be part of their developing Mediumship, both able to give communication and both loving healing energy. I experienced the power of healing in their home many times.

I was invited to stay in their beautiful home and enjoyed my time with them. We have kept in touch, and I hope we will always be friends.

We also have an incredible connection through my healing gift. On two separate occasions, when they were in need of healing, and I had asked my Healing guides to work with them, I was seen by them in their own home. Krystyna has also verified that, even after a serious operation, she had benefitted from the healing I sent. Such is the power and love of the Spirit Healers.

...

I cannot finish my Canada story without mentioning a very dear friend Kathy Topper. Kathy and her wife Carol were people I met the first time I went to the Ontario church, Kathy sometimes coming to the workshops I did, particularly the Trance workshops.

One day she invited me to have a day out with her and Carol. I love the large charity shops in Canada and Kathy did a full inventory of our day out, which was a visit to 5 charity shops, lunch, dinner at a casino, then Carol and I were allowed to try our luck at the machines later (I was only ever willing to spend $120 and invariably having bought dinner for us all I would play for about 90 minutes, coming out with the money I had gone in with)

This became a tradition, so much so that it would say on the programme for my month's visit "Day out with Kathy and Carol". Sadly, Carol became more and more ill, eventually being confined to a wheelchair and Kathy became her carer, despite having some health issues herself.

On one visit we went to a place called Orillia which was

near to the place where Kathy's mum lived. Kathy was desperate for her mum to come to live in Guelph, her thought being she would be able to look after her mum when she was an old lady. Her mum did move and Kathy was thrilled.

Sadly, shortly after this Kathy developed a very aggressive cancer, which affected all her main organs and more. She was so brave, doing everything homeopathic and natural to help herself. In the March before I was due to visit Canada, Carol went to sleep and never woke up. Kathy, naturally devastated, just knew she had to be strong for herself. Being the generous, young woman, she was she still insisted on giving me my usual day out. The strangest thing happened (Carol loved casinos, Kathy hated them but being totally unselfish, always supported Carol when she wanted to go)

We visited the charity shops but, truth to tell, our hearts were not really into it because we had always had Carol with us. We had a nice lunch and then we set off for the casino, Kathy insisting I must have my usual tradition. She had driven to this particular casino many times but, no matter how hard she tried, she could not find it.

I simply said "why don't we go for an ice cream and just sit and talk for a while", which we did. She wrote to thank me afterwards, saying she had had no idea how stressed she was, or how unwell.

In time, sadly, her cancer progressed very quickly, and she spent some of her last days in the house her mum had moved to. Pat was a wonderful help to them during the last couple of days being on duty when needed, and able to use her nursing skills as well as offering any other help they needed.

When the time came for my next visit, I feel sure Kathy had waited for me to come to Canada. We sat together in her mum's living room, she in her hospital bed, and even at that stage she was thinking of everyone else.

This was almost the end of my visit for that year. A couple of days after I arrived back in England Kathy Topper died and a lady who had lightened up the world for everyone else, was free at last from the pain and struggles she had been experiencing.

The following year when I went to Ontario Pat and I visited Kathy's mum, to help her clear Kathy's house prior to it being sold. Knowing that I do a lot of charity work to help the poor children in Africa, she told me to take anything I wanted if it would help those children. The children were very grateful because I sold some of the things and sent money for a Christmas party.

Esther is the wonderful mother of a wonderful daughter, an artist who had lived in the woods for years and enjoyed it. She moved to be nearer her daughter, never expecting she would become the carer of her much younger daughter. I write to her now, and she writes to me, we are keeping the memory of Kathy alive, the children in Africa benefitted and I was privileged to have known a wonderful person. Kathy's message to the world was simple, always be true to yourself, never complain and believe in the power of Spirit. She certainly walked her talk in this physical world and I have no doubt she is helping people now she is in the Spirit world.

...

My last visit to Ontario was in October 2019. I had received an email from the Multiple Sclerosis society, asking me would I do something for them as a fund-raiser, so of course, I agreed and said I would do them a demonstration of mediumship, for no fee, just to help their fund-raising. It was quite funny making all the arrangements because, initially the poster that was put out was on a background of a laughing skull. That was not acceptable so it had to be changed, plus there was much talk of drinking alcohol, also not acceptable during a demonstration of mediumship by a

British medium, as our standards regarding working with Spirit are very high and very respectful.

The week before I was due to go, I developed a horrific kidney infection, rarely having felt such terrible pain. I went to the doctor, was given antibiotics and then prayed the pain would go away. It did not, so I telephoned Pat and she said I should try to get there and she would look after me. I will never know how I made that trip because there was no painkiller which reduced the pain, and the only relief I had was when I had a hot water bottle on my kidney area. The staff on the plane were fabulous and looked after me very well.

I arrived and immediately went to bed and stayed there for many days. Finally, came the day of the demonstration, and by mid- afternoon all I could do was what I had done for the many days since I arrived, staying in bed and sleeping, when I could, to get some rest from the pain.

I woke mid-afternoon, and spoke very strongly to my Spirit workers, saying "If I can't do the demonstration tonight I will not want to work with you any more" This was not an idle threat. I was in so much pain and it made no sense that I had slept so much, had run out of anti-biotics yet felt no better at all.

I went to shower and whilst in the bathroom I heard a man clearly say "I had every pain you have and more. I died recently and I am a dad"

I told Pat about the conversation, she drove us to venue and I met the young lady who had arranged the evening event and her boss, another lovely lady.
When it was time to do the demonstration I finally, put down the hot water bottle and after a short introduction said that I had a man telling me he was a dad, had died recently and that he died of cancer. There was no response whatsoever! I said it again and gave another piece of evidence and someone shouted out that the recipient was

behind me so I turned round and there was the lady who was in charge of the society.

I asked if it was correct her dad had recently died of cancer, to which she said "yes" so I said "then it must be correct that he had it in the kidney, the spleen, and other organs" to which I pointed. She burst into tears and said "yes" Then followed many pieces of evidence for her until he wanted to talk about his wife, who is still living. The young lady pointed to a lady sitting at a table in front of me and said "there she is". I told her that her husband was telling me she was his back-bone and she replied "yes". Again, there were many pieces of evidential information, dates, names etc., until I could hear the sound of a motorbike. I told her that her husband had loved his motorbike to which I received an emphatic "no".

I was very confused because I could hear it, smell it and felt I was actually on a motorbike. When I gave the next piece of information the lady's daughter shouted out "mum, the skidoo!" I burst out laughing, never having heard of a skidoo.

By now most people were laughing because, apparently, a skidoo is a machine that when being ridden can feel, smell and sound like a motorbike but its particular function is to be able to go through snow, very typical in that part of Canada.

It was a wonderful evening, introducing as it did many new people to Mediumship, as many were simply there to support the Multiple Sclerosis society, and I believe we raised in excess of $3,000.
The following day I went to the hospital, was thoroughly examined, and during the next few days, slowly but surely, I recovered from the Kidney infection.

...

We never know, at the start of a journey, where we will be led and I thought maybe my Mediumistic association with

Canada had come to the end of the road, but Spirit had other ideas.

At the end of 2019 I visited Ottawa, a most beautiful city, and was hosted by the President of the church there who is also the Pastor. What an honour because her mother, a British woman living in Canada for many years, had been a working medium until she had died around the age of 100. I enjoyed the atmosphere, the way the church was run, their caring and the group I had for a workshop. Little did I know that one of the people had a sister who runs an organisation in another part of Canada. He spoke to his sister about me and said she should book me to go to her group, and as a result she had a reading with me, only afterwards introducing herself properly, telling me about her brother and inviting me to go to do a workshop for her people, something to look forward to. This proves to me that when one door closes another one is opened by the Spirit world if you work for them for the right reasons. Currently, I am negotiating with a Spiritual group in New Brunswick, as due to the current Pandemic I have had to cancel my annual visit, so my workshops will be done on Zoom, new technology that has certainly ensured the truth and message of Spirit can still be communicated.

It is truly amazing to sit in my office in England and to feel, very strongly, the connection between the Spirit person and the person having a reading, and when doing workshops, to be able to blend and bond people together as if they were in the same room.

I have re-scheduled for 2021 to visit Ontario and if Spirit will wish it to be so I will be very happy to be there. I Have also been invited to other areas of Canada and look forward to reconnecting to the good friends I have made there-My Canadian family!

DENMARK

In my first book, Two Worlds as One, I told the story of a two- page article that had been published in a Danish daily newspaper, the headline being "Telephone to the Dead" Having visited Denmark twice a year for many years, around the year 2000 I went to the organisation I regularly worked for.

Unfortunately, the female organiser became quite ill some years later, they closed the organisation and later her lovely husband died of cancer. I have wonderful memories of our times together.

During an earlier visit to them I did a demonstration in their local community centre, in their tiny village. We never knew how many people would come, or if they could speak English or not, so she was always on duty to be a translator when needed I remember giving a message to a lady, saying there was a young man in Spirit, her son, and that I could see her putting sweets on his grave. I described them and she told me that every Christmas she took those particular sweets to him as they were his favourite.

I went on to tell her that he said a little robin had come and just sat looking at her whilst she tidied up his grave, and that sometimes a robin came right up to her back door and she would simply pause for a minute to talk to it, all this proving that her son had been watching over her, very comforting for a mother who lost a child.

About four years after that I was giving a lady a message, and I had not realised that it was the same person, simply because I see so many people during the course of a year. I remembered her as I spoke to her about the sweets she put on the grave (often when we re-connect with a Spirit person, there is a vague memory coming back that we had this same link before) She said 'yes', it was true and during the course of this message her son continued to give her different evidence mentioning a visit from a robin again.

She said "yes" it had come to her just three days previously, and often it appeared, at times during the year you would not expect to see a robin, as normally you would only them in the winter months.

One amazing aspect of our association was that she came to speak to me after one of the demonstrations. She told me that she had not used the English language since she was 15 (she was now around 60) but that she had understood every word I had said.

I believe this is because there are times, when you truly are a good evidential medium, that you are able to manifest the love, personality and emotion of the Spirit communicator, allowing the recipient to feel it, and this mum obviously had experienced that, proving again that there are no language or cultural barriers to our ability to communicate with loves ones, once they have died physically I love working with young people in the Spirit world because they are always so honest and straightforward.

One connection, with a couple whose only daughter had died in a car accident, became a strong on-going link with her and she sometimes brought other people's children in to connect them to their parents during demonstrations of mediumship. I will call her Ann.

Ann's parents also had many experiences with a robin, which they also took as a sign that Ann was visiting them. Their daughter was their only child, who they had absolutely adored and they were naturally devastated when she died. However, we had many happy times during sittings and demonstrations, and they always said how much it helped. For a time, we were good friends and I would always be invited to their home when I visited Denmark.

Our friendship was wonderful, they were kind and generous people. When Ann's mum was 50, despite not wanting to celebrate, she decided to hold a birthday party, inviting her family, close friends and people who had helped her and her husband after Ann died. I was very surprised and happy, to receive an invitation to stay with them and to attend the party, which would be held in Copenhagen.

I cannot remember how many people were there, but I lost count of how many people came to me to say thank you, one man saying the party could not have happened if I had not given them such wonderful evidence of the Spiritual survival of Ann. I was very touched to know that the communications with Ann had not only helped her parents but also given so many other people an insight into truly evidential mediumship Ann became a prolific communicator, often appearing at demonstrations where her parents were. During one event she said 'Would you just tell my mum and dad I'm here, but I haven't come for them, I've brought through this young man'.
She had actually brought the young man to the mother, who I mentioned earlier, who just "happened" to be sitting in front of her parents.

On another occasion that boy came in and said that he wanted to help somebody else make contact who had never communicated a message to their loved ones left behind.

Eventually I discovered that there was connection between the parents of these children. The way Spirit children can bring their parents to each other is sometimes remarkable. Ann's parents contacted me after hearing of a message another couple had had, giving evidence of their son in Spirit. They told Ann's parents who came to a local demonstration to see me, and Ann chose to help other young people in Spirit to find the way to helping their grieving parents.

It is very important, for grieving parents to receive absolutely evidential messages from their children. Often, I give information from the past, the present circumstances and then something for them to look forward to in the

future, having established my integrity and credibility
during the initial contact we had

...

SITTINGS FOR TV

As a genuine medium, who has been tested by journalists,
the police, and scientists, as well as many people searching
for evidence of life after death, and having become known
in Denmark I was approached by a TV company, via my
Danish hosts, and asked if I would be willing to take part in
an experiment they were embarking on, the purpose being
to reach more people, who may, previously, have had no
interest in contacting their loved ones.

I agreed and they simply put an advert on the Internet,
asking for people who had never had communication from
Spirit to come forward. They would then interview them,
ask who they wished to hear from, offer them a sitting with
me, which would be recorded and then do another
interview, so the recipient could explain the relevance of
the information they had been given.
My host's home was a large house in the countryside and,
in addition, they had built a small house at the end of their
garden in which sittings, workshops etc., were held.

The experiment was set up, with camera crew and the
producer doing the pre-sitting interview in the kitchen of
the main house. I was to stay in my bedroom until called
out to the small house to do the sitting. I explained to the
producer that the best thing would be to bring me an article
belonging to the person who would be the recipient and I
would link in via my "voice" and we would take it from
there. Once I was seated in the small house the producer
would interview me and then would follow my lead,
bringing the recipient from the main house.

The first sitter was a man, who sometimes said "yes" and
sometimes nothing at all. When I had finished he leaned
forward and said, 'Now, can you just tell me something I
don't know, because I knew all of that." I burst out laughing

saying 'Where do you think I got it from? I got it from your relative in Spirit" The poor man had no clue whatsoever what mediumship was or how it worked.

When I was given an article belonging to the second recipient, by the producer I said 'Whoever this Spirit person is does not want to talk to you as a producer or you as a camera person. There are two people in the house and you must bring those people out here straight away." The two people were brought out immediately and as soon as I saw them, I said 'I've got a little boy here, he is around the age of two, and he is telling me he had a lot of pains at his head. I am feeling that this is meningitis." They said that was correct.

Then I said he was a mummy's boy, but they both said "no, you are wrong, he was a daddy's boy". So, I asked the little boy and responded to the parents 'No, when this little boy was ill, he only wanted his mummy. He needed to sit on his mummy's knee and wrap his arms around her neck and she made him feel secure. They agreed that that was correct. He gave lots of other proof and information about people in their lives now.

The real evidence came when, as he was finishing his contact, I found myself putting my hands in a curled-up position as you would if someone was going to put something into your hands. Clairvoyantly, I could see lots of coloured sweets. I did not know what they were, but they were pink and yellow and red and green and a bright sort of blue, not quite royal blue.

 I watched as the little boy took all the blue ones, one by one, and put them into his daddy's hands. The parents spontaneously, burst into tears, because his favourite sweets were M&M's and he always gave his daddy all the blue ones!!

...

The final recipient came in. I told the recipient, a man, "I have a lady, she died with cancer", then I described her in her bed." I said where the cancer was, and he said 'No, no, no'. (I believe if we are getting two no's, something is wrong and we need to ask for more information from Spirit and if we receive another "no" we should abandon the sitting)

After giving another piece of information, and receiving another "no" I said to the producer 'This just is not working, I am obviously wrong with this man, he does not understand anything I've said. I cannot deny I've got this contact in the spirit world, so I am afraid it is not going to work.' The producer was very angry, she asked questions and she said 'Can you try again but I refused and told her "I have tried to establish my integrity, the man does not understand it, so I must abandon it. "

They took the man out and talked to him in the kitchen in the main house, coming came back later to tell me 'We cannot understand it, because you established that it was his aunt, the way she died, how she was in her bed and things that had been said between them. Before he came in here, he told us those were the things he wanted to hear and that she was the person he wanted to hear from. We talked to him afterwards and asked him 'Why did you say no to it, and he responded by saying 'I don't know.' Sadly, it was of no worth and no value for television. Someone from the company wrote to me. I still have their letter, which states that though it was very good information, but they would not put it on TV because the wonderful sitting with the child and his parents was too good and it might upset people! They further said that the TV series that later went ahead (the first of its kind in Denmark) did so because they were so inspired by my evidential mediumship, so at least I paved the way for others to work there.

There was a follow up to this story. The original producer of the Programme went to work abroad. After some time, he returned to Denmark, came across the filming, watched it, and then telephoned me to say he was amazed that my footage had not been used. He further said that when he watched the reading of the parents from their little boy he actually cried.

I can only say that I believe everything is in its correct order, and that if Spirit had wanted me to be televised in Denmark, they would have made sure it happened, as it has in many other countries.

...

A SCIENTIFIC PROPHECY
I love Danish people, for their individuality, and their need to ensure everyone is happy when there.

I was very privileged to meet a truly remarkable man, who together with his wife, had researched the truth of Life after Death for many years, true researchers of Spirit communication, which I did not know when I first met them. I will call them Lise and Hans.

They had private sittings with me, came to my demonstrations and they liked my work. One evening I gave Lise a message during a public demonstration at Ølstykke Library. I said that I had a gentleman with me. I went on to describe him, and then said "he is telling me about a picture that you have that he did.' She said 'No, I do not know anything about that.' I said 'Well, I can see it, it's a boat on water, and it's a typical boat-on-water scene.' I then sort of outlined the shape of the boat etc. 'No, I don't know anything about that at all" she said.

After the demonstration Lise went home and I found out much later that when one of them had had a message from a Medium as true researchers, she and her husband always discussed in detail any information they got.

During their conversation about my message to Lisa, Hans suddenly jumped up and went running to where all sorts of memorabilia were, coming back with a postcard. The man I had been giving evidence of was a scientist who Hans had known and who had done a psychic research project with him, back in the 1980's.

One day the scientist had done a drawing when he was away somewhere, depicting the sea scene just as I described which he had sent to their daughter. They had kept it all those years, but it was tucked away and they had totally forgotten about it.

Hans recalled, that the scientist, now in Spirit, had said to him in 1984: 'One day you'll meet a very good British female medium and they will call her 'The Telephone to the Dead'.

Hans, such a lovely man, is in Spirit now and I have no doubt he is still conducting experiments and enjoying every minute. He was the most honest, generous person I knew. He never tired of investigating the truths of mediumship and The Spirit World.

Denmark and the people there will always have a special place in my heart, my work dried up for a time, mainly due to my hosts having to close their organisation, as well as so many Danish people now being mediums themselves. Also, I was told recently that a British medium has told many of the people I knew that I was ill, suggesting that I was no longer working!

Spirit obviously has other ideas. I have been asked to go back to work there, to two different places, and with 40 years of experience, love for Spirit and passion for my work I am looking forward to it very much, in 2021.

FAMOUS PEOPLE
LIBERACE
Back in the 1990's I visited my friend in Pennsylvania and while I was there was asked to do a reading for a man called Peter. I had never met him before and knew nothing about

him whatsoever. I established evidence of survival for him, from people in the Spirit world who he had known, and situations in his life that were relevant to him, all of which he verified.

During the reading I became aware of a man in the Spirit world, a very sick looking man, depicting how he looked shortly before he passed. I described him, said I could hear a piano being played, gave details of the personality of the man and then suddenly I was aware of being in a theatre in New York. The man in Spirit felt quite at home there, with an audience, and, again I could hear the piano being played. I asked Peter if it made sense as this seemed to be someone who was bringing memories to him and he asked if I knew where the man was, to which I replied honestly "no". He replied: Well, I know who he is, that was Liberace. I knew him in New York when I worked in a theatre and everything you said about him was true. Liberace was, apparently a lovely man who genuinely loved people and who never said "no" to anyone he could help.

I was thrilled but that was not the end of the story. During the sitting I told Peter that he would shortly be going on a very long trip. He said he was sure I was wrong, so I merely repeated what I was being told, and said let us wait and see. The following week my friend and I drove to Florida, many hundreds of miles away. We visited Cassadaga, a Psychic and Spiritualist village. We were sitting on a veranda relaxing when suddenly I said "I cannot believe this, look who is here!

Of course, it was Peter who I had done the sitting for the previous week. Out of the blue he had received a telephone call, a couple of days after his sitting, from an elderly friend who said she needed him to come to Florida.
So, not only did the message come true but, on this occasion, I was also able to know of it very quickly indeed.

...

FREDDIE MERCURY

During one of my seminars in the North of England I was doing readings when one my regular ladies came to me. Again, just a regular reading with a build-up of evidence, establishing my credibility, then suddenly I thought I had gone a little mad, so I stopped the reading.

She asked why I had stopped and I said "because I have obviously got something wrong". Just tell me what you heard, she said. I told her that Freddie Mercury was with me and was telling me he was helping her to write songs, to which she replied "Yes, he is" There are other people, very well known by the general public who have trusted me with their evidence and it would be totally inappropriate for me to write about them, but I will always be grateful they trusted me. Sometimes it is the need of the Spirit person to offload their issues, even if it is not possible to connect them to a loved one in the physical world.

...

THE ACTOR

I have a friendly association with a man I did readings for, as long ago as 1995, and he sometimes advises clients of his in the business world to reach out to me for a reading.
In 2018 he gave one of his clients my details and we made arrangements for him to have a reading, by Skype. On the evening of his reading I realized he had not paid, so I wrote and asked if he had changed his mind. No, he said, he really wanted the reading but had put my name in his diary without putting why it was there, so he had basically forgotten.

Again, just a regular reading, with evidential information, describing a property he said he was just renting, in the area I described, then there was a lot of information about specific matters I could not possibly have knowledge of. He verified that everything was correct, and the reading ended with communication for his wife, from her grandmother in Spirit.

He wrote to me afterwards, validating all the evidential information I had given him, and THEN came the punch-line. He sent me details of a website to show what he had, also, done in the previous 13 years.

I checked it out and felt so ridiculous that I was actually blushing. The man was a famous actor in America. I had no idea at all, and not one word about his acting career came up in the reading, so I felt very stupid!

After a while, I thought of the implications of the lack of evidence about his acting career and realized that, as apparently some so-called mediums are doing, I could have just put his name on my computer and everything he has done as an actor was there to see, including many photos of some of the people he has worked with.

If I had given him any of that information, he may have thought I had just checked him out, whereas the evidence I did give to him was not knowledge in the public domain. I was so grateful to Spirit once I realized they had been doubly clever on this particular occasion, and let us never forget that everyone who is "Famous" is simply a human being with the same sadness, grief and problems and issues as those of no fame at all, and that when they are in the Spirit world they have the same need to contact their loved ones, still in this physical world.

...

A private reading should always be exactly that, and should remain confidential. I have had contact from Royalty in the Spirit world, and more recently from a Pope, a famous actress and other well-known people.

I believe those people have trusted me because I will never write about their stories if they don't want me to – as mediums we are nothing if we do not have integrity, and I treasure and respect my own Spiritual gifts so much that I would not wish to risk losing them, neither would I abuse Spirit in any way.

TESTIMONIALS

HELLO, SPIRIT CALLING EARTH-MELISSA'S OWN WORDS.

I was told to connect with Val from the great beyond. In 2016, I had planned a trip to England to study at the Arthur Findlay College of Metaphysical Studies, the world's foremost school on psychic development. I had been there the year before and it was a transformative experience. It is a very magical and spiritual place with teachers from around the world. Weeks before I was set to leave, I was jolted from a sound sleep at 3:30 in the morning by a bubble of yellow light. From it spoke my beloved guides. "Val Williams," was all they said. So, in the dim pre-dawn light I raced to my computer and typed her name. Much to my amazement she was teaching a course at the Arthur Findlay College one week before I was scheduled to arrive! I immediately registered, changed my flight, and returned to bed.

The next morning at my office I sat with a new client. At the end of his session he told me he had readings from people all over the world and Val Williams was one of the best readings he ever had and that I must meet her. He went on to tell me how he took one of her training courses and she had changed his life.

When I arrived at Arthur Findlay I was filled with excitement and anticipation. From the moment Minister Val Williams started teaching I knew I was on my divine pathway and that she was a part of my future and of my past. At that point, I'd had many spiritual teachers, including the Dalai Lama, but Val was able to clearly outline my current circumstances, described my guides, and warned me about taking on too much. But most importantly, I discovered she was the voice I'd been hearing throughout my childhood. Starting when I was 7 years old when things were frightening to me I would hear a voice that I knew wanted to help me. The voice would say, "Hold on dear, everything will be ok". It was an energetic presence that was so safe and comforting to me and I felt like it was my fairy godmother. That first day I heard Val speak I recognized that voice from my childhood. When I told her as much, she explained that for years she would sit in meditation and send out bubbles of light and love to children around the world who were in difficult situations.

I believe that there are guideposts in this life that help us to overcome and stay the course. Val Williams has been that for me. She came into my life when I was a child and needed to feel safe and she was there for me. When we met at Arthur Findlay all those years later, I was healing my relationship with my father, as he was dying and she again helped me not be afraid and to heal. These experiences have been some of the most profound events of my lifetime. Val Williams validated who I am and provided so much compassion and helped me become the person that I am today. I am honoured and humbled to introduce to you this beautiful soul who indeed will touch you and your heart.

Melissa Boyd, Spiritual Medium

...

TIM'S TESTIMONIAL, IN HIS OWN WORDS
Fifteen years ago Val, an International medium, Minister of the Spiritualist National Union and an experienced tutor at The Arthur Findlay College was the Course Organizer of an Advanced Mediumship course at the College.

On this course she allowed a novice student, booked on the course, to continue despite the obvious lack of Spiritual attunement and uncertainty about why he was there at all. I was there because my partner at the time had decided to be there, and said it would do me good to be there too, and as it turns out she was right.

A week later, thanks to considerable effort, time and patience from Val, I was hooked and the Spirit world had a new recruit, and the task of bringing awareness of life beyond physical death. Without that initial push and inspiration from Val I would never have become what I am fifteen years later, a dedicated Spiritualist, a Spiritualist

Healing Medium, a spirit artist and trance medium, and most surprising of all, a tutor myself at the Arthur Findlay College.

I am just one of many thousands of souls across this world this surprising woman has made aware of their potential as Spiritual beings. I have met many of them over the intervening years and their story matches mine. We all owe our awareness to the determined efforts of Val Williams. Today, I consider myself a friend to Val, and on occasion have worked with her on Courses at the College as her flow tutor. She still makes it her duty to develop those with potential as attuned mediums to realise that potential. Without her drive and determination, I know many who would not have found Spirit communion, especially those of my gender who seem to need an extra push to take that leap of faith.

On mine and their behalf, I take this opportunity to thank her, a woman with a life mission and purpose. Enjoy the read

Tim Smith, Tutor at the Arthur Findlay College

...

WAYNE'S STORY

Dear Val,

I just wanted to write and thank you from the bottom of my heart for the message you gave to me at Harborne Church. It was only my second visit to a Spiritual church, and I was amazed that my father came through so soon.

I wanted to share this story with you, and why, when you said right at the end "I love you too son" it was total confirmation.

My father was always a person who thought men shouldn't hug each other, including father and son. Only once can I recall, as a child, he put his arm around me when I was ill. I always vowed that if I had a son I would always make a point of hugging him, which is what I did to an extent with my stepson.

When the news broke that my father had terminal cancer, yes, I felt totally helpless like you told me. All I wanted to do was hug him and tell him I loved him. We were like best friends so this wasn't what you normally say and do. Well, I chose my moment. It was after my cousin's wedding and he dropped me off at home. I asked him, with great unease "Dad, can I have a hug"

He replied in his usual joking way "Yes, of course you can you big soft thing" and we embraced. I had never told my father I loved him, well not as an adult, and I seized this opportunity to tell him, to which he replied "I love you too son". Not I love you, or I miss you, the exact thing you said on his behalf, and I guess he knew I would recognize this. You also mentioned that I had his wallet and there was a five pound note, possibly folded in this wallet. After the message I telephoned my mother and I told her.

She then informed me that only a few hours ago she had come across my dad's wallet. Once she had handled it and recalled some memories, she put it away in a safe place. With regards to the five-pound note: I was with my dad as a child, when he was demolishing some houses. He lifted some lino flooring and there were two old five-pound notes underneath. He kept one and gave the other to my mother, who had it framed.

During the telephone call, she told me that she had decided to hang the five pound note back on the wall in order to avoid possible damage to the frame, all this on the same day, the day of the message that you gave to me from my father.

Thank you, you really made my weekend. I've waited ten years for this special moment and I cannot thank you enough.

God Bless you,
Wayne, 8th October 2008

GARY'S STORY

Dear Val,

I was thrilled to receive a reply to the letter I sent thanking you for the message received during a service at Stansted Hall on 5th August 2001. You asked if we would consider providing a report of our experience for possible use in your next book. We would be more than happy to share our experience with your readers, you are welcome to use the original letter I sent to you. In addition, please find below our account of the communication, we are happy for you to use our names.

I first discovered Stansted Hall nearly three years ago when I went for healing to help with Crohn's disease. I had been attending Public services for about 2 years and my parents, Jean and John have been coming with me to the occasional service since the beginning of 2,000 Sadly, in March of this year we lost my brother, Gary, quite suddenly to Cancer, at the age of 49. Gary was what some would call a "non-believer" as he didn't believe in any particular Religion, though I had a conversation with him about a year ago, when he admitted to me that he had wondered if there was "something else" as he put it. However, I felt sure he would communicate one day from the Spirit world. Mum was sceptical due to Gary being a "non-believer" and Dad, after reading quite a number of books on Spiritualism was convinced Gary would eventually make contact. Dad did consider a private reading but decided he would rather continue to attend services. We began to visit Stansted Hall on a regular basis, hoping every time that tonight would be our night.

On this particular evening Dad decided that we had to sit at the front of the Sanctuary (although we know that Spirit don't mind where we sit!). So, myself, my aunt, mum and dad all sat on the front row, each of us feeling extremely emotional right from the start of the evening, as we admitted to each other after the service. We were all thinking it would be our turn next.

You were accompanied by Mike Rowlands on piano, which seemed to really raise the energy levels in the Sanctuary, creating a beautiful atmosphere. You began your mediumship by giving two messages to other people and then as we had all thought it was "our turn" you started by saying "Who has recently lost a grown-up son to the Spirit world?"

You were looking right at my parents and you then began the contact by saying that he wasn't telling you what he passed with , and that he said "it's none of your business". We were instantly convinced it was our Gary coming through as this was exactly what we would have expected him to say. You told us that he said we had been waiting for him to contact us and that he had come to tell us he had arrived safely, something he always did when he was here. You went on to tell us that he was mobile again. This was VERY significant as Gary was paralysed before he passed.

You went on to tell Mum that Gary says "don't worry about that final goodbye, if you say goodbye you can't say hello again!" This was comforting for Mum as she and I got to the Hospital just minutes after he passed and hadn't been able to say goodbye. You went on to give a message to Dad, saying that Gary knew he was worrying about losing other members of his family, and that he must stop worrying. You also passed on a message about Dad's shed that made us all laugh as this was always a point of discussion and humour between them. You also said that a lady with pin-curls was looking after him in the Spirit world and that she was cooking for him. We believe this to be my auntie Ivy (who wasn't the world's greatest cook, so this was also amusing)

I'm sure you will remember us as we were the family in tears, tears of sadness, relief and happiness all at the same time.

You said it wasn't the strongest link you had ever had but still you went on to provide us with much more evidence and personal information.

Finally, Mike Rowlands played some more music and whilst he was playing you were being urged by Gary to scrape some candle wax from the table where you were perched. This was very characteristic of him, you went on to mention that he was always tidying up just like his mum.

That evening has meant a great deal to myself, mum and dad, just knowing that Gary has arrived safely and is happy. Personally, it has been a great comfort to know that he is in the Spirit world looking out for us, and though we all miss him terribly and always will, I personally have felt more peaceful since that evening.

As I said in my first letter, August 5th in the Sanctuary at Stansted Hall was truly a moving experience for us all and one that will be remembered and treasured always by us. Thank you so much.
Jenny, Jean and John

...

CRAIG's STORY – IN HIS OWN WORDS
The first time I went to the Arthur Findlay College, I only stayed for the first two days of a week long programme. I did not really feel the connection or excitement with the programme I'd booked onto, more my own doing than that of the programme tutors or fellow students.

During lunch and dinner, I was quite open (within a small closed group) about my feelings and the kind of development I felt would accelerate me. It was here that Val Williams was recommended to me by a fellow student. I was curious to hear more.

I learnt that Val, whilst top of her game, was Northern, straight talking, VERY disciplined and no nonsense. In being honest with myself, that was just what I needed. Without hesitation I went to reception, booked onto Val's Advanced Programme and left.

Coming back to Arthur Findlay College for the second time, I was more excited. It was like the first day of school. I remember having to stand in line for a one to one with Val, where she would assess and put you into a designated group for the duration of the week.

As I approached, becoming more nervous, I could see a pair of eyes peering over the glasses taking a look as she called out "next". Before she could speak, I blurted out "I'd like to be in our group". Why she asked? "Because I need discipline". Do you indeed? She responded, dismissing me with a call of "next" and giving me the most beautiful, affectionate smile with a sparkle in her eyes.
I was placed in Val's group and have never looked back. I quickly learnt the heartfelt admiration Val has for her students. So soft on the inside, but firm (and true to her reputation) on the outside.

This is because of her dedication in delivering the highest standards of mediumship and keeping the benchmark high. In doing this Val speaks openly and honestly, is extremely patient and is like a matriarch for standards. Whilst an honour to work for Spirit, I am blessed that Spirit have brought us together and placed me under Val's mentorship as I continue to develop and grow to more effectively serve Spirit.
Craig

...

EARTH ANGELS:
JOYCE SHARPLES.
Joyce Sharples was one of my dearest friends, always there in the background of my life since I met her in the 1990's at Stourbridge church. She and Terry used to host the mediums who visited the church, but Terry was often away, working on the oil rigs.

They loved the English countryside and their final home was a little tumbledown cottage, which they rented from a farmer. It had originally been two farm-workers cottages, so goodness knows how they lived there with their families! It was very small.

Joyce and I kept in touch via letters and phone calls over the years, and each time we got together it was just like yesterday. She always signed her cards and letters to me "your spiritual sister" and truly she was like a sister to me. Joyce was one of the kindest, most giving, unselfish people I've ever met. When Terry became ill with lung disease, she devoted seven years of her life to nursing him and caring for him.

Her only outlet was her Spiritual work. She loved being a circle leader at the church and loved her public work doing services. She had become a very good medium, thanks to the West Midlands exponents programme, but, more than that, she was just a naturally Spiritual person.

We always kept in touch and when Terry was coming to the end of his life I would visit, but stay at a local motel, just so that I could take her out for lunch and offer her a little respite.

Shortly before Terry's death, I was at a Ministers Conference and, mid-afternoon I just knew I had to leave to go and see Joyce. The journey to their house was a two-hour detour, but I knew I had to visit them that particular day. I left with the kind words of the other Ministers ringing in my ears and picked up cakes on route to give Joyce a smile and a little treat.

The following week, Terry died peacefully at home. I was honoured to take his funeral at Stourbridge church, and Joyce, always a wonderful hostess, seemed to be in her element. She made sure everyone was alright, that they had enough food to eat at the reception afterwards, but I became a little worried about her, thinking that the reality

of what had recently happened had not hit her yet.
I changed my arrangements to leave after the funeral. I was due to work in the South of England a couple of days later. I told Joyce I would spend the night with her and would leave the following morning.

It was only when we got back to her house, that she realized just how stressed she was. As so many people do at the funeral of a loved one, Joyce had simply carried on as always. She was so busy helping everyone else, she forgot that she was grieving too.

During the evening, we chatted, went through photos, talked of old memories and of how, now, Terry would not suffer any longer.

It had been a long, hard battle and Joyce had had to cope o her own. It had been very isolating for her. During this time, the doctor had given her an anti-depressant, but as she became increasingly depressed and developed a lot of side effects, I asked her to try to wean herself off of them.
Joyce was on her own for only a few months when her mum became ill with bowel cancer. Her mum was over 100 years old so, of course, Joyce again volunteered to be the carer. She had her mum come to live with her, so that she could take care of her. Nurses came in and out but Joyce was permanently on duty.

There was no point telling Joyce that this would be too stressful, especially after nursing Terry for so long. She would have to do what she thought was right.

During these times of looking after loved ones, first her husband and then her mother. Joyce's only respite was going to the spiritualist church, taking mediumship classes and being in receipt of healing, which many people were sending to her.

During the time Joyce's mum was dying I was working at the College. When I was due to leave I telephoned Joyce, asking her to get a sitter for her mum and telling said that I would meet her at a pub we liked to eat at, in Worcester.

It was a bright, sunny day. I was there first and when she arrived, she looked lovely, but very tired. I had no idea this would be the last time that I would see her alive.
Shortly after this, her mother died. The funeral was held on Thursday and the family from Scotland, who had stayed with Joyce, left on the Sunday afternoon. Joyce went to church that night for the first time in a long time, and very excitedly told everyone that she was going to come to stay with me. She said that I was going to have a birthday party for her, give her gifts and generally take good care of her, which we had planned to do.

Every year, for the previous ten years, I would choose a date for her to come stay with me, according to how busy my schedule was. Whenever she came to stay, we would go shopping, sight-seeing, eat out and generally have a good time. Those weeks became very precious to both of us, and even Terry had acknowledged that she was always energized when she got home again.

Over the years, I had organised Demonstrations of Mediumship and when Joyce was with me, she would take part in them. They were always Charity events. Many times, I had to organise a funeral for someone, and sometimes I actually had to do a funeral service. Joyce never complained. She was always very proud of the spiritual work I did.

On one occasion, a 2-year-old little girl had died of meningitis. Joyce had come with me to interview the family. It was quite heart breaking, but having her with me helped tremendously.

When a good friend, Gina, died, Joyce stood in the doorway of the church and crematorium, handing out envelopes for donations. I cannot remember a time when we didn't have some good work to do for someone. Joyce would always be

there, saying, "You just do what you have to do, babe."
I still clearly remember 2014 and Joyce's annual visit. She was unwell from the moment she arrived, and, within a few hours, I had hospitalised her. Apparently, there was a problem with her gall bladder. She was truly in chronic pain. The next two weeks were terrible. During that time, she was in the hospital permanently and the doctors were refusing to operate on her gall bladder, because they'd discovered that she had a heart murmur.

Whilst in the hospital, Joyce became an Earth Angel for the older patients, even pointing out to one nurse that the elderly lady in the bed next to her had been taken off her drip and not put back on it. When the relatives came the next day, they thanked Joyce and said that they were sure that their mum would have died if it had not been for her. This was so typical of the good person I was proud to call my friend.

At the end of 2014, I telephoned Joyce and gave her a date to come to visit in August 2015. This time, it was the latest that it had ever been. Usually, it was around her birthday at the end of July.

Nevertheless, we looked forward to it and, the nearer it came, the more excited I became. Joyce was utterly exhausted. She had been put on a double dose of anti-depressants, was sleeping most of the time, and, after having looked after her mum, was feeling quite ill herself. Two weeks before she was due to visit, I told her not to bring a formal suit as she always did, in case I had to do a funeral, because as I said, "You won't need it." Little did I know the reason that she wouldn't need it!

Her bedroom was ready for her arrival, her birthday presents were ready and I had planned a belated party for her. The following day I received a phone call, the memory of which still makes my brain go numb!

Joyce's son telephoned to say my lovely friend had died in

the night, having had a heart attack. She had telephoned the emergency line just after 1am, and when the paramedics finally arrived, over an hour later, she was dead.

I have never lost a child or a partner, but I can only imagine what that pain is like. I truly felt as if my heart would explode.

How could it be that my lovely friend, who had given everything of herself to everyone else for sixty-seven years, have passed so suddenly just when, for the first time in her whole life, she was free to enjoy herself and pursue her love of mediumship?

It's easy to say that she should have taken more care of herself, that she should have come off the anti-depressants (something I still believe) and that she should have asked other people to help her more. None of that brings her back to us, does it?

I just hope her grandsons will remember her as the most amazing grandmother who ever lived. She was always ready to talk to them and to console them. She was very proud of them, having told me her eldest grandson was going to teach her computer skills.

She will always be in the mind and heart of those who knew her. Nothing negative could be said about her, her spiritual nature or the love she gave to others.

If you ever visit Stourbridge Spiritualist church, please go into the peace garden where you will find a beautiful bench, created by someone who loved Joyce. It is a lasting memory which honours a very special lady.

She is happy now, I am sure, watching over us, and making sure we are all safe. My life is all the better for having known her, although I still miss her every day.
I took her funeral service during the days that she would

have been staying in Blackburn with me, so the timing was absolutely right. I just did not know the reason I chose those particular dates at the time. Spirit always knows best, though, and perhaps it is a good thing that we don't always know what is just around the corner?

This year, around the time that Joyce would normally visit, I went into the guest bedroom (Joyce's room) and picked up a lamp I had bought, so that she could read in bed. It flickered on and off, and then would not go on again, so I just had to leave it and use another light. Of course, I said to Joyce, "If that is you, please find another way of letting me know you are around." The lamp has worked perfectly ever since.

I am surprised not to have had more messages from Joyce in the twelve months since she passed, but I did have one that was very evidential. It came from a young woman giving one of her first ever messages, on her first seminar. She said she had to give me a message from my sister (my immediate thought was that I don't have a sister in Spirit, but I kept quiet.)

She said my 'sister' was sitting on a very pale green sofa (mine is that colour) and that she was very comfy and that I was very stressed and should sit there more often. She further said that my 'sister' was now stretching out full length and looked very much at home, then gave me a short message from her.

What an incredible message, delivered so simply. Joyce always sat on my sofa every evening, rolling her cigarettes for the following day, and when she had finished she used to stretch out full length.

The message was truly evidential from my point of view, and as I have said so many times, sometimes the best evidence is given from people new to their own spiritual development. Thanks to Joyce for continuing to be my 'spiritual sister.'

A year after Joyce had died, her grandson had tried to contact his dad, who was Joyce's only child. As he could not get hold of him, he went to his dad's house, but sadly found that he too had passed to Spirit. Now Joyce has with her the beloved son she always worried about so much.

It is normal to question why these things happen, but we will never find all the answers. Sometimes, we may just have to accept that everything is in its right order, no matter how painful it is at the time.

...

ANNE ENGLISH

As Joyce taught me to be a better person so did a very special lady called Anne English. Anne lives in Portsmouth and has hosted me for the Spiritualist church there ever since my lovely friend, Lotte, died several years ago. Anne is, without a doubt, the most amazing lady. She's had no children of her own, but treats everyone around her as family. She is kind and generous, and always puts everyone before herself.

She has nursed many members of her family, taking care of them with the utmost love and patience. Most recently, Anne took care of a gentleman who was terminally ill and had stayed in her home for the length of his illness.

Her amazing Spirituality could be a lesson to many, myself included, and I can honestly say that she taught me to not be afraid of giving to people whose need is greater than mine.

I was brought up in the 1950's, when there was never enough money for treats or pocket money or the things that children nowadays automatically expect and have. When I began to earn my own money and had to buy my own clothes, I remember having just one dress, even when I was pregnant! I could only afford one dress and had to wash it overnight each night to wear the following day.

During my marriage, my husband earned very little. Somehow, I always managed to pay the bills and we had no debt. In those days I was not "allowed" to work and it was easier to give in to keep the peace.

After my marriage ended and I began to earn my own money, it was vital that I should not be in debt of any sort. The very thought of debt petrified me, so I was very careful that if I could save a little I would do so, and this continued until, thanks to my father, I was able to pay off my mortgage and have my home just as I needed it to be. From that time, I cautiously saved a little, because as a self-employed person working as a Medium there can be no guarantee that there will be enough work to pay the bills and life has certainly taught me that lesson.

During the years that I've been in my current home, on two separate occasions I found myself unable to work, due to health issues. It was Anne who insisted on helping me by paying my utility bills until I could work again, Anne who hosted me in her own home for extra days when I went to serve the church, and Anne who, during my association with her, has never refused to help anyone in need. In fact, she is always one step ahead, discreetly offering support, visiting people, doing shopping for them and listening for hours on end to their worries and problems.

I do not use the words 'Earth Angel' lightly when I talk of Anne, because she is the person who taught me not to be afraid of reaching out to others who need help, and not to be afraid of giving a little of my own money to someone who desperately needs it. She is one of our world's unsung heroes, working away quietly in the background, doing healing on whatever level it is needed and moving gently from one person to the next.

'Ah,' I hear you say. 'She is very lucky, she must have had an easy life.' Quite the contrary, I can assure you. Instead of complaining about her own sadness and stress, she has harnessed it in such a way that she can genuinely show

empathy to those she meets in her every- day life.
Every-one of us can do a little something to help someone else, whether that help is by giving money, goods, time or something as simple as spending two hours every afternoon with an elderly relative, who has dementia, but still loves to play scrabble, for example.

When my friend, Lotte, died, it was Anne English who wrote to me to say there would always be a bed for me in her home and she has more than lived up to her word. I am very grateful that Spirit brought us together and for her loving friendship.

...

LINDA CARR
The name, 'Linda Carr,' to those who knew her is synonymous with strength, bravery, humour, kindness, encouragement, etc. I could go on and on, simply because every-one who ever met Linda would have their own story to tell.

I first met her when I moved to Rotherham in 1989. She had come to see me do a demonstration at the church and, shortly afterwards, we formed an association, that later became a respectful friendship.

When Linda had met her husband, John, they instantly fell in love, married and had one son whom they adored. When their son was very young, they were all in a car together, when they were involved in a terrible accident. Tragically, that accident left Linda paraplegic. The doctors said that she would never walk again and, initially, that she would remain in a vegetative state.

Linda, however, had other ideas. John told me that every time he visited her at the hospital, she was black and blue, because she was determined to walk, but kept falling.

She did, in time, walk with the use of a frame, and went on to do physical things that many of us would not have dared try, pushing herself as far as physically possible. My first memory of seeing her working was at Rotherham church again and I remember that she had to climb some stairs to get up to it.

She really was an inspiration. On a much later occasion, I remember that we went to a Chinese restaurant in St. Anne's on Sea, which had a double set of stairs. She got up the stairs on her bottom, saying 'nothing would stop her, and nothing could!!!

Linda's family were not Spiritualists, but John's were. He had mediumship in his teenage years, but chose not to pursue it as a young man. Linda was taken by her mother-in- law to the churches and became an exceptional medium. By the time I met her, she was in constant demand to do services and demonstrations, as well as private sittings, for which she would not charge any money. She said she did not need to, but one day we had a long discussion, during which I pointed out that she was not being fair to other mediums in the area and that if she charged a little it may be of benefit to them. We also discussed that she often helped people pay for seminars etc., so perhaps she could put any money people gave to her towards that or even to the seminars she attended.

On some occasions, I asked her to work on my courses at the Lindum hotel, in St. Anne's on Sea, and other times she simply booked in, to enjoy the pleasure of being with like-minded people.

She became very well known throughout the country for her mediumship and, in later years, for her trance and physical mediumship.

No one who knew her would have dared to suggest to Linda that she was disabled, even though she had no feeling, other than pain, in her legs. I never heard her complain and when I spoke to John, he verified that she never complained, even though she was in constant discomfort.

In the background of seminars, in her own home and at local Spiritualist churches, Linda helped countless people with the natural emotions and problems that arose during early stages of development. She always gave her time freely.

In 2004, Linda attended my annual seminar and she reminded me of a conversation we had had two years previously, during which she had told me that her spine was going to "snap" in the place that was damaged in the accident and that she would be paralysed. I asked her if she had told John and in typical Linda fashion, she said, "No, I don't want to worry him."

Two years later, the situation had become much more serious and she told me that she would have to go into hospital shortly after the annual seminar.

At the end of the weekend, I asked if she would like to have some healing and I can honestly say it was one of the most special times I have spent with Spirit. She had said that she would like to have healing, so we formed a circle of people, with Linda and I in the middle of it. All who were sitting around the circle then offered their energy, to become part of her healing process.

I remember going into a very deep altered state, probably for 15-20 minutes, and as I came out of it I could clearly hear myself saying, "And should you reach a state when your life is no longer acceptable to you, we will take you very gently into the Spirit world" At this point, she screamed very loudly and burst into heart-breaking sobs. Her friend sitting opposite from her comforted her and then said, "Linda, the Spirit guide just answered every question you've been asking, because you told me what you had asked."

It was heart-rending and humbling at the same time, to have been allowed to become such a special part of Linda's process at that time.

We said 'good-bye' the following day and little did I realise that it actually was goodbye.

During the following nine weeks, I travelled both at home and abroad with my work for Spirit. Everywhere I went, I would think, 'On Wednesday, 16th June 2004, I will go to see Linda in Sheffield.' I had no idea at the time that it would be the day that I would do a funeral service for her! I received a phone call during my week at the Arthur Findlay College to tell me she had passed to Spirit and to ask me if I would take the funeral service at what had been her local church in Sheffield. Darnall Spiritualist church was where she had worked tirelessly for the committee, taking classes and doing other good works, to help them whenever necessary.

I immediately telephoned my good friend, Barry, to ask if he would put together a brochure for the service. Linda was known as our Purple Lady, her favourite colour, so I wanted to have everything in the service that she would have liked if she was around to choose.

On the Saturday morning, as I was preparing to leave the College to drive to Grimsby, where I was to work at the church there that weekend, I telephoned Barry and he told me he could not find lilac paper for the cover of the brochure. I quickly ran into the College office and asked if I could borrow some and would replace it the next time I worked there. There were 110 pieces and I needed 100!

John came to Grimsby to discuss the funeral service, but before I saw him, Linda came to me and said, "I can wear my nice shoes now." As soon as John arrived, I told him this. I said to him, "Surely, you have not taken shoes to the funeral director for her?!" He burst into tears and explained that he had bought her a lovely pair of shoes, which she had loved, but had not had the opportunity to wear. He had, indeed, just taken them to the funeral director! (The following day, John telephoned me to say that I had taken away 75% of his grief, with just those few words.

We organised the funeral service together. It is always very important to get everything just right for our loved ones, to make the service a celebration of life.

It was a beautiful service. It was everything that Linda would have wanted. All of her friends and family were there, sitting in the church that she had served for so long. One of the ladies who was on the committee of the church even organised food for after the service. All of the men were wearing lilac shirts and all the women wore lilac or purple in Linda's honour and memory.

John had wanted the coffin to be open and had arranged for Linda to wear a new suit he had bought for her on their last holiday together. Almost everyone in the church came onto the rostrum to say their last goodbye to their special lady.

After the service, we were to drive from Sheffield to Rotherham crematorium and as John, Tom and I took our places in the car carrying Linda, I turned to Tom, the son Linda loved so very much and said, "Three people heard your mum sing during the service," to which he replied, "Val, I heard my mum sing during the service!"
For those who did not know Linda, when she did a Trance demonstration, she had a variety of guides who would make their presence known. At the end of the demonstration, one guide would always come through, who had apparently been a black slave .He would bring her back to physical consciousness by singing the song, 'Swing Low, Sweet Chariot' in a deep, resonant voice, something that you never forgot once you had heard it. I chose this song as a surprise for her family as part of Linda's funeral service. Linda's loving connection with us has continued. I arranged a memorial service at my annual seminar the following year, to which John came. He brought our friend, Freda, because Linda had asked him to take care of her. He has been to every annual seminar since and is as loved as Linda was, by everyone who has met him. Linda will never be forgotten. She had the loudest laugh and loved to make an entrance when we had fancy dress discos. She was a truly Spiritual lady, always available for anyone who needed her

and I know that she is continuing her progression the Spirit world, in her own special way.

I know, for a fact, that she is currently helping people who are developing their Mediumship. As a mentor in her physical life, she was great at encouraging people to just be who and what Spirit wanted them to be. She was solid, down-to-earth and honest at all times. What you saw was what you get, as we say in the North of England, and she is, and will always be missed.

A couple of years after she died, I was taking a class at the Arthur Findlay College and encouraging people to truly be in the power of Spirit before they stepped forward onto the little stage in the Lecture room.

I will never forget what happened. A wonderful medium called Austyn Wells from the USA, was on the course. She stood up and looked as if she was struggling, literally pushing one leg in front of the other. She struggled to get on to the rostrum and then said, "Now I am where I belong." She had quite perfectly manifested the Spirit of Linda Carr. I was able to telephone John afterward and I know this brought him great comfort.

To this day, whenever I am at the College taking classes, she manifests to one of the students during the week and I often have to call John to verify the evidence.

So, her legacy of helping developing mediums is continuing and we are happy to know she has found her rightful place in the Spirit world. She was definitely an Earth Angel, and is now continuing in her life in Spirit.

If you visit Stansted Hall, The Arthur Findlay College, there are many benches in the grounds with plaques in memory of those who are now in Spirit and there is one for Linda, someone we will never forget.

...

JUNE BROWN.

Over 20 years ago June and I met on a seminar I was working on, and she came as a student, though already working with her mediumship when she had time.

She was a remarkable lady who worked very hard, was a pharmaceutical manager, a very intelligent lady who used her intelligence when it came to Mediumship, always testing, always searching.

She and I became good friends and had many friends in common.

Sadly, she developed cancer, was very brave, had all the treatment necessary, and refused to wear a wig when her hair fell out due to the treatment.

One day, having been cleared of the cancer (she was told) she attended a church where she was a regular attendee, and as she sat waiting for the service to start she told me later, her vision changed and she saw, Spiritually, a coffin being brought in ready for a funeral. I remember her telling me she thought immediately "that is me in that coffin" How very distressing for us all but mostly for June, when some months later she developed chronic pains in her back. I felt quite sure this was the cancer developing in another area, but simply suggested she go to see her doctor. At first her doctor seemed not to wish to examine her or check it out but she insisted, and yes, indeed, she had cancer which became increasingly debilitating and painful as it went into her bones.

This time she was unable to fight it, though she was incredibly brave, but each time she had treatment she was worse in health in every way. Ultimately, she did die and she did have her funeral in the very church she had had her vision.

Thankfully, she had had so many opportunities to work with her mediumship that she had no doubt at all that there was a Spirit world and that one day she would be re-united with her loved ones. She was one of the people I call Earth Angels and I feel sure she is now continuing her pathway of progression by helping those of us left behind in our physical world.

AUGUST 2018 GITTE DIED.
Gitte was one of the most wonderful women I ever met, positive, funny, and inspirational. She and her husband, Prebn, became very good friends of mine. Gitte and I met when she came to a workshop I was doing in Denmark in the early 1990's, and later she came with other Danish people to my annual seminar in the North of England. She enjoyed being there, despite one of the other Danish people being very unkind to her, and we struck up a friendship there and then.

Sometime later I discovered that she and her husband created music and songs together, entertaining large crowds in hotels and other venues.

I had needed somewhere to record my meditation CDs and was told Prebn had his own recording studio in his garage at home, so the next time I was going to Denmark I contacted him and he has done all the recordings and presentations of my CDs ever since.

It was fun going to record them at their place and Prebn said he was very impressed used as he was to dealing with musicians. Apparently, he was not used to seeing someone come in, put ear phones on, talk for 20 minutes, finish, go to the bathroom, come back, put on the headphones again, do another 20 minute meditation and then simply finish. I explained to him that every word was inspirational. He never charged me any money for the recordings, used to give me a finished master copy, and then I brought each one home to England and had them copied in the Midlands, beautifully produced and professional copies.

The organisations I worked for closed one by one until there was no work for me in Denmark but we always kept in touch.

I used to find nice outfits for Gitte in Canada and sent them to her, glamorous evening jackets and nice trousers, to wear for her musical entertainment performances with Prebn. As soon as she received them, she would e mail and thank me, except the last time in July 2018.

As I had not heard from her I e-mailed to ask if she had received the latest jacket. On August 27th she telephoned me but I could not understand anything she said, sounding as if she had had a stroke.

I could not contact her by phone when I tried so eventually wrote to her, by mail, and asked her to ask her grand-daughter to let me know what was happening.

Shortly after I received a short e mail from her husband, simply saying she had died 4 days after she telephoned me. Have you ever been so shocked because someone was such an amazing personality that you never considered they would no longer be in your life? That is how Gitte's death made me feel, shocked and bewildered.

Of course, very quickly my thoughts turned to her lovely husband, as they had so adored each other, laughed together all the time and just enjoyed being together. Again, I thought the Spirit world is lucky to have welcomed her home but we will all miss her.

LYNETTE

My final Earth Angel, for this book, is a lady I considered to be a friend, someone I loved very dearly and who, by the way she lived her life, proved that Spirit can help us to cope with everything.

Lynette was certainly tested, and passed every test! She had a spinal condition which meant her spine was no longer straight and her body was quite bent (she told me she loved to do martial arts, so I knew straight away there was something special about her)

I first met her at the College. She had booked for a seminar and there were not many students at all. The ones who were there each had a very specific need to be on this particular week, each one testing Spirit at the time for a variety of reasons.

One day I asked Lynette to open our session with a prayer and I can say it was the most beautiful prayer I ever heard. The words resonated with everyone for our individual needs.

She also manifested an excitement, a respect for Spirit that was quite unique and she loved, above all, the healing aspects of our Spiritual work.

A jeweller by profession, together with her daughter Annette, she sometimes made a piece of jewellery which could be used to raise funds for charity. One day she contacted me to say she and Annette had made a piece of gold, which I could raffle for any charity of my choice. I was totally overwhelmed when she told me it was worth over £500!

At the time a young friend was dying of cancer so I thought the best way to use it would be to sell raffle tickets, all proceeds to be given to the trust fund for my friend's children.

I got a license from the local council, had special tickets printed, added a couple of other prizes, and we raised a huge amount of money. Lynette was thrilled.

Sadly, for all who knew her, Lynette broke her neck in a freak accident. I received a call to tell me she was in hospital in a critical situation and rushed to visit her as soon as I was able.

What happened during the following 9 months was, for those of us who knew her heart-breaking but, at the same time, quite awe inspiring. She never complained about what had happened to her (her only complaint was she hated the hospital food)

On one occasion I visited her with a friend, we called at Marks and Spencer. I remember it was Easter and she had sent her family on holiday, to give them a break. I never saw anyone so excited about beetroot salad!

Each time I visited she would say "I know I am learning something from this, but I don't know what the lesson is". Some days when I visited, we talked about some of the Spiritual experiences she was having, all bringing her closer to those in the Spirit world.

A wonderful healer, herself, I was happy to have had the opportunity to sit in her home, in her healing circle, and to have seen what a wonderful grandmother and mother she was, truly her daughters best friend.
When she died, I cried for days, not for her, but for myself and all the people who would miss her. I think we often cry for ourselves, at the same time being very happy our friends and loved ones are no longer suffering.

She has left us a great legacy: accept what is happening, never to feel we are being punished, just know we have a lesson to learn.

If I could have a wish granted it would be to be as genuinely accepting as she was of everything that life had thrown at her.

She has left her daughter, who she adored, and a son-in-law who gave her the greatest gift of all, a beautiful grand-daughter, truly an English rose, growing up to be the nicest young lady and I know Lynette will always watch over her.
I am grateful to all of these special people I have known, each of whom taught me something special. It is my

greatest joy when they come back via another medium to give a little love and a little reassurance, always when it is needed the most.

HELLO, I'M STILL AROUND.
LUKE & LUKE-February 2020
I have said a thousand times that Spirit have surprised me so many times I cannot be surprised again, well guess what? This past week has been the most remarkable one I can remember for a long time.

Three weeks ago, a friend's son passed to Spirit, aged only 44, a horrible experience for everyone but I believe, particularly for a parent. After all no child should die before their parents should they? It always seems to be in totally the wrong order, and no matter how many times I encounter this, through the blessing of being able to connect young people in Spirit to their parents in the physical world, I thank God that this did not happen to me.

Some weeks ago, a friend, English but living in Spain, recommended me to a couple from Yorkshire. Tony had been in touch and I could not quite fit in a time that seemed right. Eventually, I sat with my diary, chose a date and sent it to him on e-mail. He said it suited him but he was not sure if it would work for his wife. I explained that I would prefer to see them separately if they did both come and this was acceptable to him.

The day before the appointment he e-mailed to say his wife would be coming with him.

I started tuning in to Spirit half an hour before they were due to arrive and, as I stood at the top of my stairs, I had a terrible pain over my left eye that got worse within seconds, spread up into my head and then I had a horrible sickly feeling, and a feeling I could not see out of my left eye. As I moved to go downstairs, I felt dizzy and had to hold on to something to stop myself falling.

They duly arrived half an hour early and I said I would prefer not to have them in together, so Tony's wife went away for half an hour.

As I walked into my living room, where Tony was sitting, the pain I had had a few minutes earlier built up again, and I was aware of the presence of a young man. I asked Tony if it was correct that he had lost a child, a boy, to which he replied "yes". I explained the pain and asked if it made sense in relation to his son and he said "yes" again. His son came really close and I was able to give enough evidence to prove to him I really was connecting with his son.

Tony's wife then arrived and he said he would like to sit in on her sitting. I felt that was alright but after five minutes I had to ask him to go. Although his son had told me how much he loved both his parents he wanted to have time alone with his mum. Tony immediately said he would go away and come back in half an hour.

The sitting then became incredibly loving, emotional and evidential all at the same time, an almost perfect connection, but I still did not have his name. This often happens, so I don't worry about it too much.

After the sitting we talked and she said his name was "Luke" and that I had really brought her son's wonderful personality alive. Apparently, he died because he had a brain tumour, which explained all the pain, eye problems etc. that I had felt before the sittings began.

We said goodbye after I asked would it be alright to use his name in a book I was writing, originally with the help of a young woman. His mum laughed and said he would absolutely love it. He was a gregarious, out-going, happy young man and loved to be the centre of attention.

Before she left Luke's mum asked me what he would be doing in Spirit, so I explained that young people (he was 26) usually bonded together in Spirit and did everything they could to help each other to connect to loved ones who are still living.

This whole week has certainly proven this to be true!

...

At this stage I was to tell the story of another young man called Luke, who had died tragically, who came to give someone beautiful evidence which the young lady said had truly helped her healing process. Suffice to say the reason that Spirit had wanted her and I to meet had been fulfilled, and once this was done there was no need for further contact with each other.

She came into my life, as I said earlier, offering to help to write my book with me. Sadly, it did not work out, despite many hours put in by both of us. I am now totally rewriting my original script.

I will always be grateful to Spirit for connecting us, so her young man, in Spirit, could make contact with her, obviously the real reason for us meeting.

...

THE MOTORCYCLIST

I have a friend called Sara, who is a nurse. She is very down to earth, practical and sensible. For some time she had regularly been having a dream in which she dreamt that her son was screaming out to her for help, a recurring nightmare causing her to be on duty, constantly waiting for the phone call to actually come.

Sara understands Spirit and Mediumship, and I have, on occasion, been to her home to do private readings for her and friends.

Sara's son, Mathew, had two best friends, Andrew and Paul. I had met one of the friends in the past as well as his mother. I had not heard from the group for some time, though I periodically saw Sara, then one evening she telephoned and asked if I would go to her home and do reading for three or four people.

It was May 2013, a time never to be forgotten I know now! I arrived and was taken to the room where I was to do the readings. As soon as Andrew came in the room, I told him I had a young man, in Spirit, who had died on a motorbike. Andrew was unusually quiet throughout the reading, pretty much saying nothing in response.

When he left his mum came into the room and, again, I told her I had a young man, in Spirit, who had died on a motorbike. She seemed a little upset but did respond at times, just saying "yes" or "no".

Finally, Sara came into the room and, again I said I had a young man who had died on his motorbike, then without thinking I said "Oh, my God, there was a decapitation". Sara burst into tears. I carried on with the reading because I did not want to lose contact with Paul, explaining to her that I needed to continue to give evidence from him.
When I had concluded the reading Sara and I talked for a while because, as I said to her, I had no idea it was the same young man during the first two sittings, but during hers, it became obvious it was.(due to the differences in relationships, the personality of the Spirit person can seem to be different also)

Apparently, what had happened was that Paul had just passed his test on his motorbike, so Mathew and Andrew said that they should all go out on their bikes for a practice run. Andrew's girlfriend was on the back of his bike.

They had set off with Andrew in the lead, Paul following and Mathew at the rear. There was a series of roundabouts, and just after they left one Andrew had gone ahead, Paul lost control of his bike and crashed into the central barrier, bouncing off it many times. He was thrown from the bike losing his helmet and when Mathew reached him it was totally devastating.

There was blood pouring from the carotid artery, Mathew was holding Paul's head, and at the same time telephoning his mum, Sara, screaming for her to help him! (Yes of course, as she had heard many times in her nightmares) A witness to the accident telephoned for an ambulance, and the emergency services responded as quickly as possible.

Some weeks later I invited Sara and her friend to my home to sit in a circle, to link with Spirit, not for any particular reason, or so I thought.

During the evening Paul came to me and said he had not finished giving his information when I met with him last. Distressing though this was for everyone involved, the mere fact that Paul had tried to communicate directly with these two ladies was very meaningful to them. Paul had recently "come out", confiding to his closest friends Mathew and Andrew that he was gay, knowing his own family would not accept that at all. His best friends had always known, nothing changed. They had been, and would always have continued to be, best friends, and Paul always felt very much at home at Sara's house, she being his second mum. Shortly after this I was the course organizer for one of my annual weeks at the Arthur Findlay College, the course having many people from different parts of the world as always.

One of the students during the week was a lovely lady from Italy, who told me one day that she had had a visit from a boy in Spirit, when she was in her bedroom. I will never forget her words, as she described a gorgeous, dark haired young man, who was very funny, but she said "all I had of him was his head".

The lady told me she had always had experiences of a psychic nature but she had no idea she was actually a medium until she came on this particular course. I was so thrilled she had come on my course, if only so she could give this wonderful message, that a young man loved by so many, who had died so tragically, was able to communicate his survival of death to her!

I contacted Sara immediately and she sent me photos of Paul, the Italian lady confirming that was who she had seen, all of this being very reassuring for Sara, who by then was very worried about her son Mathew.

Mathew found it, understandably, very difficult to erase from his mind what had happened, he helping his best friend as he was dying. For anyone to have such an experience it would be difficult, heart-breaking, and nightmare inducing but, for a young man in his early 20's it was just too difficult. For some time, Sara was frightened her son would never recover from everything and in the deepest emotional sense he probably never will BUT I met him recently and we were able to talk about Paul's death for the first time.

The pain is still obvious to see when you look into Mathew's eyes but then we never do forget what has happened, we simply learn to live with it. Mathew did become like a lost little soul for a time but now, 7 years since the incident, he is reassessing his life, moving forward and hopefully accepting that Paul is getting on with his new life in the Spirit world.

Andrew and Mathew will always be friends, bonded by the love of their friend Paul and no doubt they have a maturity that many people years older than they don't have. Sara will never forget the lovely boy she knew but, having researched mediumship for many years she knows that Paul is now happy, and she can ask him to help her son to be happy also and I absolutely know Paul will help him. I thought that would be the end of the story but I decided to go to the Lindum hotel for a few days in August, to finish the book and get away from my own home for a total break. Sara telephoned me and when I said where I was, she asked if I like her to come to stay for an overnight visit.

Lovely, I thought, planning to work very hard, and then cut off on Friday. She arrived early afternoon, we had a chat, lunch, a nap and in the evening, I did a service on Zoom for Windsor church.

As I woke on Saturday morning, I was very aware of Paul's presence and my "voice" told me I should offer to do a reading for Sara, as she had been through such a lot of personal stress during the previous 7 years. She was thrilled so after breakfast I did her the reading, during which Paul came, with so much to say, messages for Mathew, and he spoke about how he was teasing Mathew.

Sara and I then went shopping, had lunch and came back to the hotel to collect her luggage. Mathew telephoned her to say a tin of foam he used for his work had burst out all over the inside of his van, immediately Sara said that would be Paul teasing him.

In my usual down-to-earth way, I said perhaps the heat of the day had caused it to happen, but in my heart and soul I do believe it was Paul doing everything he could to make Mathew smile and doing something to prove to him that they can still be in touch with each other.

...

2020-THE END OR THE BEGINNING?
I mentioned earlier in this book that many people experienced difficulties in 2018, and were praying that 2019 would be better, only to find it was worse. This, then, made everyone wish for 2019 to be over because of course 2020 would be better.

My question is: what have you learnt during 2020? This has been, for everyone, a year that has taught us that we can never take anything for granted again, a time during which many have not been able to feel safe and secure, due to job changes or losses.

More than anything, it has been a year for people to know

what their priorities should be, and with the inability to be in touch with family or friends, with the lack of human contact, with people dying without loved ones being by their side most of the people I have discussed this with are realising that there will, when we are allowed, come a time when we will not take our loved ones for granted, that parents, though stressed and very busy, will want to spend more time with their children.

During this year, and already we are approaching September, as I look back I realise I do actually enjoy my own company and that I need more time to think about what is most important. For almost 40 years I have become busier and busier, and for every single opportunity of travelling the world, establishing life-long friendships and relationships, I will be eternally grateful to those in the Spirit world who guide and teach me, and to every person who has ever used me to pass on their message of love to someone in the physical world.

I was a child of the new world, born in 1948, the year the National Health Service came into being, During this year of the Pandemic where a virus threatened the whole world, I have never been more proud to be British, because our NHS has been magnificent and there has been a general feeling of people giving to others, taking time for others, reaching out to total strangers. All our front- line workers have given tirelessly to everyone they have helped.

At the beginning of this year a very dear friend, who I consider to be as close as family, was so very ill he was half an hour from death when he was admitted to the hospital, and I called upon every physical person I knew to send healing to him, and to every Spirit person for love, help and support to make him well. The results were absolutely astounding, thanks to our Health service and to the Spirit healers, here and in the Spirit world. Three months after he was admitted to hospital, and having been released in record time he received a phone call to say "your heart has healed itself" and while he is still tired and in recovery, there is no doubt whatsoever that, for him, 2020 is a time of a new start.

So, I wonder, when we get to the end of this year, and to the end of the Pandemic which has, in many ways restricted our lives, will we complain about what we didn't do or be grateful for what we could do?

Do you believe that Spirit knew this was going to happen? I do, and in some way I am happy I did not know in advance because I would have thought I could not cope with all the changes, cancellations, and rebooking that has had to be done, as well as the restrictions that have been placed on us all.

My over-riding feeling is of a totally new beginning, having had time to assess my life, and consider possibilities I had not had time for prior to this year.

I have finished the book that was started 10 years ago, have had time to research 40 years of photos, letters, publicity articles etc., that have been stuck in boxes for years. I have, on reflection, a much greater gratitude to the Spirit world than I had before, because when I got caught up in simply being busy I forgot the wonderful way the Spirit people weave a thread through our lives, ultimately proving that we are ALWAYS in the right place and it is ALWAYS the right time for whatever lessons we are to learn.

I have done funeral services that were, in many ways, quite heart breaking, many people not being allowed to attend loved ones' funeral services. Like so many other people who have taken such services I did the best I could to make each service a Celebration of the life of the deceased person. I hope there will be many memorial services when we are all allowed to get together again, those bringing emotional closure to so many people.

Our Spiritualist churches and Spiritual centres had, without exception, to be closed, so many people feeling lost and afraid because they always felt they needed the support they received from the churches and the committee people who give their time voluntarily to keep our meeting places open.

Like many people I felt it necessary to reach out to people, using that modern concept called Zoom, something I have been too afraid to use in the past. I enlisted the help of people who were more experienced, who had offered to help, and together we were able to meet via Zoom for healing groups, and it was obvious that the Spirit workers were happy to use this means of reassuring people. This, in turn, took away a lot of the loneliness from the people who could not physically meet their friends and fellow Spiritualists.

There were times this year, that I, too, felt sad, lost and alone, so in typical fashion I became The Born again Housewife, posting silly things on Facebook, which people have said really helped them to get through and cheered them up, and I cheered myself up by writing them.
We are, as human beings, strong and resourceful and always able to cope when we have no choice. As people who know we can connect to the Spirit world and receive support from those who have gone home to Spirit before us we KNOW we do no need to be alone with our sorrow and stress.

As I come to the last chapter of this book I know, without question, that for me this is the end of the chapter and that another book is waiting to be written.

I also know that I have gained more confidence and faith in myself this year, due to someone I met towards the end of last year. His name is Craig and he came to a seminar as a student of mediumship. He heard people asking me to mentor them, something that people have asked me to do for many years and which I have always refused to do, believing other people could probably do it better.

Thanks to his faith in me and offering to help I have finally started something which Gordon Higginson and other mediums told me I would do over 30 years ago. I was given many messages saying I would have my own sanctuary one day, and my own school for Mediumship.

I am thrilled to say that, thanks to Craig, I have started The Val Williams Academy for Mediumship (the word Academy being considered to be more modern than school) and since I agreed to do it the Spirit World have been very interactive on my behalf and on the behalf of future students.

Due to modern technology many people may want to continue to have readings and classes through Zoom but, for me, there is nothing more wonderful than to be in the presence of those developing their Spiritual gifts and having the hands-on opportunity to help them, facilitating on behalf of their Spirit Guides and teams of Spirit Workers and Teachers.

For those who wish to develop their natural mediumship there should be opportunities not only to get help with their mediumship but also to understand how difficult it can be for them as their mediumship and blending with Spirit increases their sensitivity. I believe we need to help our future mediums to be prepared for the many pit-falls they may encounter, and my Spirit team are certainly on duty, always, to help the next generation of mediums, as I was helped by some of the wonderful mediums I knew when I started my journey of development in 1980. Although totally trained by Spirit I was encouraged by people like Gordon Higginson, Ivor James, Albert Best and Don Galloway, all natural mediums, and many more who I met at the Arthur Findlay College, which is a beacon of light for Spiritual workers and a great place to come together with fellow students on this journey of Spiritual development. Whatever you have learned during this past year I pray you will know that those in the Spirit world will always help you if it is your intention to work for Spirit, for the right reasons. This book has been written by me, edited by someone else, totally re-written, proof read by three different people, all because the young woman who offered to help in the first place was derogatory about my last chapter, calling it "drivel" and "like a sermon". Her reason for saying this? Because, in her own words, SHE needed recognition and praise, and she was upset because I gave praise to Craig. She had no idea I was preparing a glowing testimonial to her, for the effort she had put into my book.

She was very scathing about it being MY book and sent me two pages of her version of an introduction, which had nothing to do with Spirit or this book, but which was entirely about herself!

For three days I was in a state of shock, bewildered by her vitriolic words, asking Spirit to help me to understand what was happening. I vowed the book would not be published! Thanks to the loving help and encouragement of friends, who assured me that they wanted to read the book, validating my right to tell the stories in my own way (many of which she had changed), saying they wanted to "hear your voice" as they were reading it.

This book was never about ME. It was always meant to be a compilation of true stories, hopefully told in a way that would help many of the people reading it.

As someone who has been "put down" for most of my life, Spirit rescuing me and proving to me I am worth something, I am telling this part of the story in case someone reading it feels exactly the same. We are all unique, and as such, we all have true worth.

For those who try to be special by using other people I would simply say – find yourself, be yourself, and let that be enough.

I realise, now, that every book that closes and every year that ends is an opportunity to open up to future possibilities and I leave myself safely in the hands of those in the world of Spirit who have always known, better than I do, what I need.

I will continue to do classes, workshops and demonstrations of mediumship on Zoom, for countries around the world and am also looking forward, very much, to working at home and abroad, in person, for all the organisations who have asked me to work for them in the past and who have booked me for future events.

Thank you for being part of my journey. I pray you will find Spiritual companionship as you look forward to opening a new chapter of your life. Remember all that you learnt as other chapters closed behind you.

There is yet another story to be told, but it is still in progress. It follows up a promise Spirit made to me many years ago. When I divorced my then husband I was co-owner of a house. The day I went to court I refused to go into the courtroom and fight for more money than he offered me. My solicitor was angry, bewildered and very upset, saying he could get me many more thousands of pounds.

I explained to him that I could not go into a court and tell the story of his abuse towards me because the following Sunday I was to take a service in a Spiritualist church. During the service I would be talking about love, Spirituality etc., following the guidelines of our wonderful Seven Principles. At that point my voice clearly said "We will replay you for this one day". This year that promise has been kept in the most amazing way.

Much of this book has been about Synchronicity. My move to a beautiful home by the sea, provided by the loving help I was promised by Spirit in 1987, will coincide with the publishing of this book.

The delays I have experienced in writing it were meant to be. The difficulties we have all experienced during the

Corona virus pandemic experience have been challenging, upsetting, frustrating etc. We will all be happy to return to whatever "normal" is.

The full story of my move will be told at a later time, in another book. Once again the people in the Spirit world have surprised me, and continue to do so every day. I cannot wait for the next chapter of my life to unfold.
I was challenged to demand from Spirit why the Corona virus had come from nowhere, what was the purpose of it. Quite frankly, if Spirit wanted us to know all the answers I know we would have been told!

As a medium I have no doubt, whatsoever, that those minds of intelligence in the Spirit world are acting, as they did 100 years ago, using at that time Spanish flu to remind us that materialism has overtaken our thinking, and that, Spiritually, we have become lost again. Our churches were full to bursting in those days and Mediums and Mediumship were vital to so many people.

Our loved ones, our guides and helper in Spirit, will help us through this time, reminding us that other people may be more in need than we are. I know so many people who have risen to the occasion, who have put others before themselves.

We have been given time to reach out, to progress spiritually, if we can just "hang on in there". As so many people have said "This, too, will pass"
To everyone who has helped me, guided me, loved and encouraged me, whether from the Spirit world or the Physical world I simply say "thank you from the bottom of my heart"

...

Printed in Great Britain
by Amazon

62374595R00088